DATE DUE

JAN 0 2 2013		
APR 2 2 2013		

Demco, Inc. 38-293

1st EDITION

Perspectives on Diseases and Disorders

Obsessive-Compulsive Disorder

Heidi Watkins
Book Editor

GALE
CENGAGE Learning

Detroit • New York • San Francisco • New Haven, Conn • Waterville, Maine • London

GALE
CENGAGE Learning

Christine Nasso, *Publisher*
Elizabeth Des Chenes, *Managing Editor*

© 2010 Greenhaven Press, a part of Gale, Cengage Learning

Gale and Greenhaven Press are registered trademarks used herein under license.

For more information, contact:
Greenhaven Press
27500 Drake Rd.
Farmington Hills, MI 48331-3535
Or you can visit our Internet site at gale.cengage.com

ALL RIGHTS RESERVED.
No part of this work covered by the copyright herein may be reproduced, transmitted, stored, or used in any form or by any means graphic, electronic, or mechanical, including but not limited to photocopying, recording, scanning, digitizing, taping, Web distribution, information networks, or information storage and retrieval systems, except as permitted under Section 107 or 108 of the 1976 United States Copyright Act, without the prior written permission of the publisher.

For product information and technology assistance, contact us at

Gale Customer Support, 1-800-877-4253
For permission to use material from this text or product, submit all requests online at www.cengage.com/permissions

Further permissions questions can be e-mailed to permissionrequest@cengage.com

Articles in Greenhaven Press anthologies are often edited for length to meet page requirements. In addition, original titles of these works are changed to clearly present the main thesis and to explicitly indicate the author's opinion. Every effort is made to ensure that Greenhaven Press accurately reflects the original intent of the authors. Every effort has been made to trace the owners of copyrighted material.

Cover image copyright Voronin76, 2009. Used under license from Shutterstock.com.

LIBRARY OF CONGRESS CATALOGING-IN-PUBLICATION DATA

Obsessive-compulsive disorder / Heidi Watkins, book editor.
   p. cm. -- (Perspectives on diseases and disorders)
  Includes bibliographical references and index.
  ISBN 978-0-7377-4791-1 (hardcover)
 1. Obsessive-compulsive disorder. I. Williams, Heidi.
  RC533.O2642 2010
  616.85'227--dc22

              2009045226

Printed in the United States of America
1 2 3 4 5 6 7 14 13 12 11 10

CONTENTS

FOREWORD

"Medicine, to produce health, has to examine disease."
—Plutarch

Independent research on a health issue is often the first step to complement discussions with a physician. But locating accurate, well-organized, understandable medical information can be a challenge. A simple Internet search on terms such as "cancer" or "diabetes," for example, returns an intimidating number of results. Sifting through the results can be daunting, particularly when some of the information is inconsistent or even contradictory. The Greenhaven Press series Perspectives on Diseases and Disorders offers a solution to the often overwhelming nature of researching diseases and disorders.

From the clinical to the personal, titles in the Perspectives on Diseases and Disorders series provide students and other researchers with authoritative, accessible information in unique anthologies that include basic information about the disease or disorder, controversial aspects of diagnosis and treatment, and first-person accounts of those impacted by the disease. The result is a well-rounded combination of primary and secondary sources that, together, provide the reader with a better understanding of the disease or disorder.

Each volume in Perspectives on Diseases and Disorders explores a particular disease or disorder in detail. Material for each volume is carefully selected from a wide range of sources, including encyclopedias, journals, newspapers, nonfiction books, speeches, government documents, pamphlets, organization newsletters, and position papers. Articles in the first chapter provide an authoritative, up-to-date overview that covers symptoms, causes and effects, treatments, cures, and medical advances. The second chapter presents a substantial number of opposing viewpoints on controversial treatments and other current debates relating to the volume topic. The third chapter offers a variety of personal perspectives on the disease or disorder. Patients, doctors, caregivers, and loved ones represent just some of the voices found in this narrative chapter.

Each Perspectives on Diseases and Disorders volume also includes:

- An **annotated table of contents** that provides a brief summary of each article in the volume.
- An **introduction** specific to the volume topic.
- Full-color **charts and graphs** to illustrate key points, concepts, and theories.
- Full-color **photos** that show aspects of the disease or disorder and enhance textual material.
- **"Fast Facts"** that highlight pertinent additional statistics and surprising points.
- A **glossary** providing users with definitions of important terms.
- A **chronology** of important dates relating to the disease or disorder.
- An annotated list of **organizations to contact** for students and other readers seeking additional information.
- A **bibliography** of additional books and periodicals for further research.
- A detailed **subject index** that allows readers to quickly find the information they need.

Whether a student researching a disorder, a patient recently diagnosed with a disease, or an individual who simply wants to learn more about a particular disease or disorder, a reader who turns to Perspectives on Diseases and Disorders will find a wealth of information in each volume that offers not only basic information, but also vigorous debate from multiple perspectives.

INTRODUCTION

"Kenneth Lang, Jr. simply couldn't throw anything away—not trash, not feces, not dogs. Not even the dead ones."[1] So opens an article in the *Detroit Free Press* from the summer of 2009. Investigators had found 260 Chihuahuas in Lang's home, 110 alive and 150 dead, stored in the freezer.

The phenomenon of animal hoarding has received increased attention in the last decade or so, as reports like this one have made shocking media headlines, but the number of actual incidences seems also to be increasing. The Animal Legal Defense Fund, emphasizing the suffering of the animals, estimates that up to 250,000 animals per year are victims and that reports of cases have been significantly increasing. A 2009 report published by *Clinical Psychology Review* reports that an estimated three thousand people per year are directly affected by animal hoarding and that reported cases increased by five times from 2000 to 2006.

What is going on? How can this happen? Why does it happen? Media reports commonly point directly at or at least mention obsessive-compulsive disorder (OCD). Estimates of people with OCD who hoard range from 18 percent to 42 percent, and most people who hoard also have other OCD symptoms. However, while OCD and hoarding, including animal hoarding, are related, the relationship is not so straightforward.

Neither animal hoarding nor hoarding in general are diagnoses recognized by the *Diagnostic and Statistical Manual of Mental Disorders, Fourth Edition* (*DSM-IV*); in other words, they are not recognized mental conditions in and of themselves, nor do they automatically

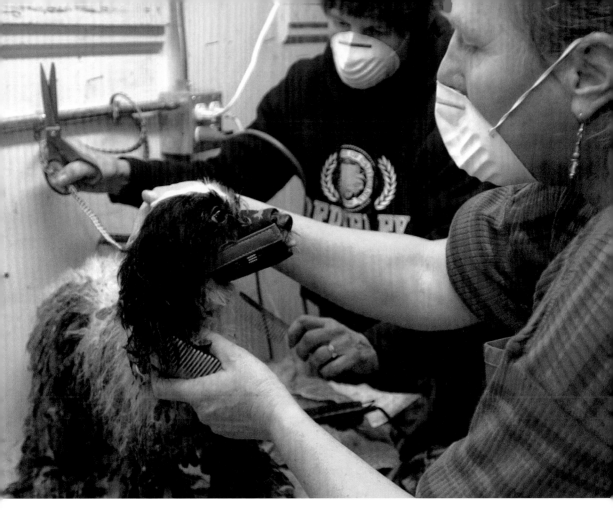

Humane Society volunteers clean the stench from a dog found in an animal hoarder's home. Of people with OCD, 18 to 42 percent may also be hoarders. (Kim O'Conner/MCT/Landov)

indicate OCD. They are listed alongside many other possible *symptoms* of OCD in the *DSM-IV*. However, hoarding is also mentioned as a symptom of many other conditions. An article published in the *Psychiatric Times* in 2007 explains that traumatic brain injury, tic disorders, mental retardation, and neurodegenerative disorders are also symptomized by hoarding.

Delusional disorder is another possible explanation for animal hoarding. In one study examining animal hoarding as a form of delusional disorder, all the animal hoarders in the pilot study vehemently believed that they could communicate or empathize with animals in a special way. Additionally, they believed that they were taking good care of their animals even when clearly they were not. An example of delusional thinking is reported on a Web site devoted to the topic of animal hoarding: Standing in three inches of feces, breathing acrid ammonia in the air, and in plain view of dead and dying dogs, one woman said, "I never hurt any dogs, I love my babies. The fact is I am protecting them."[2]

Other explanations for animal hoarding proposed by researchers include: early signs of dementia, citing that as many as 20 percent of patients diagnosed with dementia hoard some kind of objects; an addiction, on the grounds that shared characteristics between animal hoarders and addicts include being preoccupied with animals, feeling persecuted, denying that they have a problem, and neglecting themselves and their living conditions; and an attachment disorder in which relationships with pets are substituted for human relationships.

With so many other possible explanations for the behavior of animal hoarders, while tempting, it cannot automatically be assumed that people who hoard animals do so because of OCD. However, as with OCD or any other medical and/or psychological condition, understanding what causes hoarding is absolutely necessary. Successful treatment depends on it.

Because of the criminal nature of animal hoarding—neglecting animals is a crime—understanding animal hoarding is especially important. For example, the lawyer for Kenneth Lang Jr., the man found with 110 live and 150 dead Chihuahuas in his home, insists that criminal charges—felony animal cruelty charges—are not appropriate in this case due to lack of intent. "We're talking about criminal charges, and he needs therapy. There's no intent here,"[3] he claims, and goes on to say that since childhood, Lang has had OCD, has held only odd jobs, and has received disability checks for about twenty-five years.

On the other hand, animal rights groups such as Animal Rights or Human Responsibility (AR–HR) would strongly disagree with Lang's lawyer, one representative stating: "'Animal hoarding' is being labeled a mental illness, often with a reference to the DSM-IV which is the Diagnostic Standards Manual used by certified Psychologists and Psychiatrists across North America. There is a problem though. It's a lie. Animal hoarding is not a recognized diagnosable mental illness with the DSM-IV."[4]

Amanda I. Reinisch, in an article appearing in *Canadian Veterinary Journal,* recognizes this attitude, stating, "Mental health agencies, social services, and public authorities are often unable or unwilling to assist in animal hoarding cases because the animal hoarder's behavior is excused as simply a lifestyle choice and, therefore, not a public health issue."[5]

The anonymous statement of a frustrated sister of a woman who hoards animals verifies this reality and also demonstrates the complicated nature of the disorder:

> My sister fits the profile of a hoarder who is close to a major meltdown. She has about 80 dogs, 13 cats, puppies, pregnant dogs, a house in disarray, a severe recurrent depression, post-traumatic stress disorder, a borderline personality disorder, and our family is at the end of energy and resources. I have talked to all available physicians, my sister's social worker, psychiatrists, veterinarians, etc. Now I am disappointed that I have found very little help to change this situation.[6]

Clearly animal hoarding is a complicated disorder with many possible causes and, therefore, unclear solutions. Animal hoarding, in fact, may be a form of obsessive-compulsive disorder, but even as such may have different causes, demand different therapies, and require different medications to be cured or helped.

Obsessive-compulsive disorder is often stereotyped as extreme neatness, excessive hand washing, and fear of germs. Animal hoarding is only one possible form of OCD that breaks that mold; many other manifestations exist. *Perspectives on Diseases and Disorders: Obsessive-Compulsive Disorder* explores many of them as well as other controversies surrounding the disorder.

Obsessive-compulsive disorder is often characterized by excessive neatness and fear of germs. (© Bubbles Photolibrary/Alamy)

Notes

1. Amber Hunt, "Dearborn Man Who Hoarded Live, Dead Chihuahuas Not a Criminal, Lawyer Says," *Detroit Free Press,* July 27, 2009.
2. Animal Hoarding, "Inside Animal Hoarding." http://animalhoarding.com.
3. Megha Satyanarayana, "Chihuahua Owner Got Disability but Not Aid," *Detroit Free Press,* July 26, 2009.
4. E. Saunders, "Animal Hoarding: Fabricating and Criminalizing Mental Illness," Animal Rights or Human Responsibility, http://ar-hr.com/2009/03/25/animal-hoarding-fabricating-and-criminalizing-mental-illness.
5. Amanda I. Reinisch, "Animal Welfare: Understanding the Human Aspects of Animal Hoarding," *Canadian Veterinary Journal (CVJ),* vol. 49, December 2008.
6. Gary J. Patronek and James N. Nathanson, "A Theoretical Perspective to Inform Assessment and Treatment Strategies for Animal Hoarders," *Clinical Psychology Review,* vol. 29, 2009, pp. 274–81.

CHAPTER 1

Understanding OCD

An Overview of Obsessive-Compulsive Disorder

Carol A. Turkington, Helen M. Davidson, and Jacqueline L. Longe

Carol A. Turkington, Helen M. Davidson, and Jacqueline L. Longe are medical writers and editors. Additionally, Turkington has written for *Time* magazine and was the senior clinical psychology writer for an American Psychological Association magazine. In this encyclopedia entry, the writers define and describe obsessive-compulsive disorder (OCD) and explain that OCD is different from other compulsive behaviors such as gambling and substance abuse because with OCD the compulsions, such as repeated hand washing or hair pulling, bring no pleasure to the patient.

O bsessive-compulsive disorder (OCD) is a type of anxiety disorder. Anxiety disorder is the experience of prolonged, excessive worry about circumstances in one's life. OCD is characterized by distressing repetitive thoughts, impulses or images that

Photo on facing page. Some people with OCD have a constant obsession with washing their hands. (© Bubbles Photolibrary/Alamy)

SOURCE: Carol A. Turkington, Helen M. Davidson, and Jacqueline L. Longe, *Gale Encyclopedia of Medicine.* Belmont, CA: Thomson Gale, 2007. Copyright © 2007 by Thomson Gale. Reproduced by permission of Gale, a part of Cengage Learning.

are intense, or frightening, and that are unusual or not reasonable. These thoughts are usually followed by ritualized actions that can be either bizarre and irrational themselves, or can be perfectly reasonable actions, such as cleaning or hand washing, that are taken to extremes. These ritual actions, known as compulsions, help reduce anxiety caused by the individual's obsessive thoughts. Often described as the "disease of doubt," the sufferer usually knows the obsessive thoughts and compulsions are irrational but, on another level, fears they may be true.

Description of the Disorder

According to the National Institute of Mental Health, approximately 2.2 million American adults have obsessive-compulsive disorder. The number of children affected with the disorder is not clear; however, the Obsessive Compulsive Foundation reports that 1 in 25 Americans will experience OCD at some point during their lives. It can occur in children and adults. In children, symptoms often begin to appear around age 10 and in adults symptoms most commonly appear around age 21. According to the Obsessive Compulsive Foundation, up to one half of adults with OCD say that it began in childhood. Men and women are believed to be affected by OCD in approximately equal numbers. OCD affects people of all ethnicities.

It can be many years before an individual with obsessive-compulsive disorder is diagnosed. This is because individuals often try to hide their problems for fear of being labeled. Individuals with OCD are not in any way "crazy," but have repeating thoughts and fears that are so distressing the individual cannot avoid acting on them. Individuals with OCD may recognize on some level that their fears are not rational, but find them so overwhelming that they are unable not to act upon them.

Most people with obsessive-compulsive disorder have both obsessions and compulsions, but some people have just one or the other. The degree to which this condition

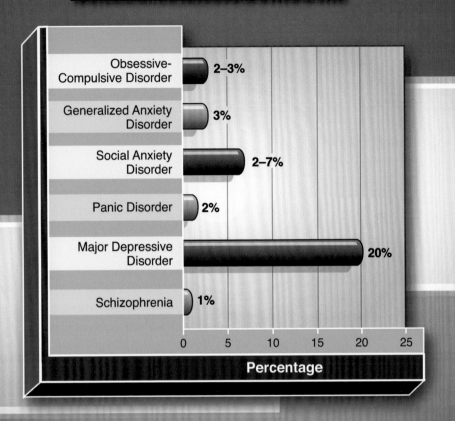

Prevalence of Obsessive-Compulsive Disorder

Disorder	Percentage
Obsessive-Compulsive Disorder	2–3%
Generalized Anxiety Disorder	3%
Social Anxiety Disorder	2–7%
Panic Disorder	2%
Major Depressive Disorder	20%
Schizophrenia	1%

Percentage

Taken from: Naomi A. Fineberg, Sanjaya Saxena, Joseph Zohar, and Kevin J. Craig, "Obsessive-Compulsive Disorder: Boundary Issues," *CNS Spectrums*, vol. 12, no. 5, 2007.

can interfere with daily living also varies. Some people are barely bothered, while others find the obsessions and compulsions to be profoundly traumatic and spend much time each day in compulsive actions.

Obsessions are intrusive, irrational thoughts that keep popping up in a person's mind, such as "my hands are dirty, I must wash them again." Typical obsessions include fears of dirt, germs, contamination, and violent or aggressive impulses. Other obsessions include feeling responsible for others' safety, or even the repeated thoughts that the person injured someone in a traffic accident when that is not the case. Additional obsessions can involve excessive religious feelings or intrusive sexual thoughts. The individual may need to confess frequently to a religious counselor or may fear acting out the strong sexual thoughts. People with obsessive-compulsive disorder may have an intense preoccupation with order and symmetry, or be unable to throw anything out.

Compulsions usually involve repetitive rituals such as excessive washing (especially hand washing or bathing), cleaning, checking and touching, counting, arranging or hoarding. Often, a person with obsessive-compulsive disorder is driven to perform the rituals because of a fear that if he or she does not, something dreadful will happen. As the person performs these acts, he or she may feel better temporarily, but there is no lasting sense of satisfaction, completion, or safety after the act is performed. Although performing the compulsions may temporarily ease stress, this short-term comfort has a very high cost. A large quantity of time spent repeating compulsive actions can significantly interfere with activities like school and work, can put a significant strain on relationships, and not leave time for the individual to pursue other activities.

The difference between OCD and other compulsive behavior is that while people who have problems with gambling, overeating or with substance abuse may appear to be compulsive, these activities also provide pleasure to some degree. The compulsions of OCD, on the other hand, are never pleasurable.

OCD may be related to some other conditions, such as the continual urge to pull out body hair (trichotillomania), fear of having a serious disease (hypochondriasis), or preoccupation with imagined defects in personal appearance (body dysmorphia). Some people with OCD also have Tourette syndrome, a condition featuring tics and unwanted vocalizations (such as swearing). OCD can occur alongside depression and with other anxiety disorders.

Causes of OCD

Research suggests that people who have a family member with OCD are more likely to develop obsessive-compulsive disorder themselves. Although no gene for OCD has been identified, it is believed that there may be a genetic predisposition that can be inherited. No one is certain what causes OCD; however, there are several theories that have been suggested. Some experts believe that OCD is related to a chemical imbalance within the brain that causes a communication problem between the front part of the brain (frontal lobe) and deeper parts of the brain responsible for the repetitive behavior. Research has shown that the orbital cortex located on the underside of the brain's frontal lobe is overactive in OCD patients. This may be one reason for the feeling of alarm that pushes the patient to perform compulsive, repetitive

OCD may manifest itself in trichotillomania, the continuous urge to pull out body hair.
(© Rob Wilkinson/Alamy)

actions. It is possible that people with OCD experience overactivity deep within the brain that causes the cells to get "stuck," much like a jammed transmission in a car damages the gears.

This could lead to the development of rigid thinking and repetitive movements common to the disorder. The fact that drugs which boost the levels of serotonin, a brain messenger substance linked to emotion and many different anxiety disorders, in the brain can reduce OCD symptoms in many patients may indicate that OCD is related to decreased levels of serotonin in the brain.

Scientists believe there may be a link between childhood episodes of strep throat and the development of OCD. It appears that in some vulnerable children, strep throat (infection with group A beta-hemolytic streptococcal pharyngitis) may precede the onset of OCD symptoms. Some scientists hypothesize that this occurs because the antibodies (cells that the body produces to fight specific diseases) that fight strep throat may act on the brain in ways that cause problems with the way neurons communicate. When this happens OCD may result.

Diagnosing OCD

People with obsessive-compulsive disorder may feel ashamed of their problem, may try to hide their symptoms, and may avoid seeking treatment for many reasons. OCD may become more severe as time goes on and it goes untreated, and more severe OCD may be more difficult to treat successfully. OCD may be frequently misdiagnosed or not diagnosed at all. According to the Obsessive Compulsive Foundation, there is an average of 17 years that elapse between the time the OCD symptoms begin and the time appropriate treatment begins. The foundation also reports that individuals with OCD usually see 3 or 4 different doctors while seeking treatment.

There is no blood or other test that can determine whether or not an individual has obsessive-compulsive disorder. Instead, doctors must obtain and assess detailed information about an individual's symptoms and history, and may even talk to friends or relatives of the individual to try to obtain as much information as possible. Only after the doctor assesses all the information gathered can a diagnosis be made.

Treatment

Obsessive-compulsive disorder can be treated by cognitive-behavioral therapy, medication that regulates the brain's serotonin levels, or a combination of both. Drugs that are approved to treat obsessive-compulsive disorder include fluoxetine (Prozac), fluvoxamine (Luvox), paroxetine (Paxil), and sertraline (Zoloft), all selective serotonin reuptake inhibitors (SSRIs) that affect the level of serotonin in the brain. Older drugs include the antidepressant clomipramine (Anafranil), a widely-studied drug in the treatment of OCD, but one that carries a greater risk of side effects than some other available drugs. Drugs may need to be taken for 12 or more weeks before it is possible to determine if they are effective for the particular individual.

Cognitive-behavioral therapy (CBT) helps individuals learn new ways of thinking, helping them end the obsessive thought patterns and learn new ways to cope with their fears that do not involve performing the compulsive rituals. Over time, the obsessive thoughts can be reduced, compulsive activities can be stopped, and the individual can spend more time doing enjoyable activities. Times of stress may increase an individual's worry or need to perform rituals, but cognitive-behavioral therapy also provides individuals with techniques to help them make it through such times.

In a few severe cases where patients have not responded to medication or behavioral therapy, brain surgery may be tried as a way of relieving the unwanted symptoms.

> **FAST FACT**
>
> Occurring at higher rates than schizophrenia, OCD may be equally debilitating and is associated with higher rates of suicide.

Surgery can help up to a third of patients with the most severe form of OCD. The most common operation involves removing a section of the brain called the cingulate cortex. The serious side effects of this surgery for some patients include seizures, personality changes, and decreased ability to plan.

Alternative Treatment

Because OCD sometimes responds to SSRI antidepressants, a botanical medicine called St. John's wort (*Hypericum perforatum*) might have some beneficial effect as well, according to herbalists. St. John's wort is prescribed by herbalists for the treatment of anxiety and depression. They believe that this herb affects brain levels of serotonin in the same way that SSRI antidepressants do. In about one out of 400 people, St. John's wort may initially increase the level of anxiety. Homeopathic constitutional therapy can help rebalance the patient's mental, emotional, and physical well-being, allowing the behaviors of OCD to abate over time.

Prognosis

Obsessive-compulsive disorder is a chronic disease that, if untreated, can last for decades, fluctuating from mild to severe and often worsening with age. When treated by a combination of drugs and behavioral therapy, most patients experience a significant reduction of symptoms, and some patients go into complete remission. Unfortunately, not all patients have such a good response. Some people cannot find relief with either drugs or behavioral therapy. Hospitalization may be required in some extreme cases.

OCD Can Be Debilitating

Jeremy Katz

Jeremy Katz, a literary agent and men's health and sports writer, wrote the following article for *Men's Health* magazine. Having wondered if his own obsessive-compulsive personality traits have contributed to his career success, he interviews Michael Jenike, medical director of the Obsessive Compulsive Disorders Institute. Jenike explains that while many OCD cases portrayed by television actors and sports figures are quirky and perhaps even seem cool, more than half of all cases are severe and can significantly impact a sufferer's quality of life. Katz's own case was troubling but relatively mild and was successfully treated with medication.

I sit in the glass-walled nurses' station, waiting for my day to begin. A steady stream of people—all living with obsessive-compulsive disorder, or OCD—approach the half door and utter some variation of "I have to go to the bathroom." The attractive young woman on duty smiles and hands over a small quantity of

SOURCE: Jeremy Katz, "Are You Crazy Enough to Succeed?" *Men's Health,* July 2008, p. 150. Copyright © 2008 Rodale, Inc. Reproduced by permission.

toilet paper, a squirt of soap in a specimen cup, and a paper towel with a cheery "Here you are!" This is what grade school must have seemed like to George Orwell [British author of the novel *1984*, which characterized a regimented society].

Pretty soon I have to go, too. How could I not?

I'm here to interview the doctor, not seek treatment from him, so I'm directed empty-handed to a staff bathroom in which I discover four separate soap dispensers, a forest of paper products, and two signs about washing my hands—one to remind me to do it, and the other to tell me how.

I'm at the Obsessive Compulsive Disorders Institute (OCDI), a residential treatment center in McLean Hospital—Harvard's psychiatric center—to see if my own OCD problem wasn't just my secret but maybe also the secret to my success. All my adult life, intrusive thoughts have alternately halted my progress and saved my ass, and I'd finally like to separate the bad from the good.

The Agony of OCD

The medical director at the center, Michael Jenike, M.D., is both a maverick and a pioneer in the OCD community. He founded this facility, the first of its kind, to help sufferers of what he considers the most agonizing of psychiatric disorders.

"I had a 17-year-old who had kidney cancer that was going to kill him in 5 or 6 months. He also had a bad case of OCD. He said he'd rather get rid of his OCD and live only 6 months, than get rid of the cancer and live with the OCD. That's when it first hit me: This is some serious stuff."

The people seeking treatment at OCDI do not have the minstrel-show version of the disorder acted out by Tony Shalhoub in *Monk* or Jack Nicholson in *As Good as It Gets*. The institute's residents are seriously impaired. They have the kind of shattering anxiety that would make the rest of the OCD world—roughly 1 percent of all

Actor Tony Shalhoub's portrayal of a detective with OCD in the television series *Monk* has led to an attitude that OCD is cool, when it is in fact a debilitating disorder. **(AP Images)**

adults, 2.3 million of them in the United States alone—want to scrub their hands. The real numbers could be even higher, because OCD may be underdiagnosed and undertreated. Half of all OCD cases are serious—and that's the highest percentage among all anxiety disorders. On average, people flail about for 17 years and see three or four doctors before they find the right care.

The Fascination with OCD

That horror aside, OCD has become cool. Perhaps it fascinates us because it forces otherwise normal people to carry out insane acts—acts that they know are insane. It has great dramatic tension. We secretly enjoy the dissonance of a perfectly rational man becoming convinced that he is fatally contaminated and washing his hands with bleach and a scrub brush, only to repeat the whole routine 10 minutes later. Paging Lady Macbeth [who tries to wash invisible, imagined blood from her hands in Shakespeare's *Macbeth*].

And anyway, who wouldn't want a condition [soccer star] David Beckham has, even if it is his signature brand of mental illness? The popularization of the disorder has led to a heap of confusion. Everyone I know is "obsessed" or "compulsive" about something. And then there's the throwaway excuse of our times: "Oh, that's just my OCD."

The Confusion About OCD

This casual imprecision only adds to the confusion of talking about OCD. Sanjaya Saxena, M.D., an associate professor of psychiatry and behavioral sciences at the University of California at San Diego and the director of the school's OCD program, points out that "the meanings of 'compulsion' and 'obsession' as we speak of them in common parlance are not the same as the strict mental-health definitions." Obsessing about your work or your girlfriend doesn't mean you have OCD, and most people understand that "compulsively" keeping a neat desk or managing a stock portfolio is no big deal.

More to the point, those everyday fixations do not put you in danger of developing full-blown OCD. Even habits that are worrisome and possibly progressive, such as sex addiction, compulsive gambling, or overdrinking, fall within the spectrum of addictive behavior and not OCD.

True OCD Is Not Rewarding

Like our common, everyday infatuations, says Dr. Saxena, these habits persist "because they are rewarding in and of their own right." A true obsession, though, is "a

Severity of New-Onset Cases of Obsessive-Compulsive Disorder (OCD)

A 2001 study conducted in 19 clinics in northern California determined the severity of symptoms in patients having new-onset OCD, as shown below.

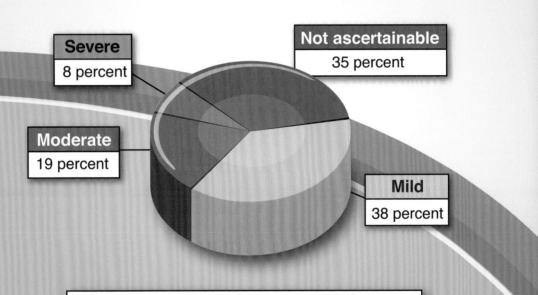

Severe
8 percent

Not ascertainable
35 percent

Moderate
19 percent

Mild
38 percent

Mild: Symptoms occupied up to 2 hours per day, caused only mild-to-moderate distress, and slightly interfered with role functioning.

Moderate: Symptoms occupied between 2 and 6 hours per day, caused moderate-to-severe distress, and interfered substantially with role functioning (subject could still meet most responsibilities).

Severe: Symptoms occupied more than 6 hours per day, were very disturbing, and caused the subject not to perform, or to perform very poorly.

Not ascertainable: Unable to be determined.

Taken from: Bruce Fireman, Lorrin M. Koran, Jeanne L. Leventhal, and Alice Jacobsen, "The Prevalence of Clinically Recognized Obsessive-Compulsive Disorder in a Large Health Maintenance Organization," American Journal of Psychiatry, November 2001, pp.1904–10.

recurrent, intrusive fear, impulse, or image that is distressing and anxiety-provoking," he says, while a compulsion is "a repetitive behavior done in response to an obsessional fear or worry and designed to prevent something bad from happening or to reduce distress."

If the behavior produces pleasure or a reward—even a strange or unhealthy reward—it's not a real obsession or compulsion, and it won't develop into one. Gerald Nestadt, M.D., a professor of psychiatry at Johns Hopkins, puts it this way: "The alcoholic may say, 'I shouldn't drink, but I love to,' whereas the person with a contamination obsession would say, 'I don't want to wash my hands, and I wish I could stop.' The reason the addictive person wants to stop is only because of the consequences, not the unwanted urge.". . .

The Doubting Disease

We all have intrusive thoughts. They flash unbidden across our mental JumboTrons, startling us with their violence, depravity, or just outright weirdness. I'd bet every New Yorker has imagined hip-checking [bumping] some stranger into the path of an oncoming subway car, and that every Californian has considered, for one brief moment, the idea of plowing his SUV into the jerk in front of him on the Santa Monica Freeway. For a person living with OCD, thoughts like these are not wadded up and tossed in the recycling bin. Instead, they are pored over, analyzed, and scrutinized for truth.

Imagine this: You've just parked the car. You hop out, grab your bag, and head toward the gym. But wait. Did you lock the car? You head back to make sure you did. Yup, it's locked. Problem solved. Jeff Szymanski, Ph.D., OCDI's director of psychological services, explains. "Someone with OCD says, 'I went and checked the car, but did I really check it? I'm looking at my hand turning the key in the lock, but is that perception really clear enough? Did I hear the click, or do I just remember hearing the click, or did I hear the click last time I checked this?'"

Shrinks call this pathological doubting, but the person with OCD doesn't need a memo from the Department of Justice to know it's torture.

A Personal Experience with OCD

Looking back, I realize that my OCD began to appear during my senior year of high school, if not earlier. I became convinced that every girl I dated was betraying me . . . nightly. And so I quizzed them on their whereabouts and demanded alibis for any unexplained absences. Oddly enough, my girlfriends found this suffocating.

My condition confined itself to that strange little corner of my world throughout my college years, and I did just fine. There are some tolerant females out there, let me tell you. But after I graduated, found a job, and moved to New York, I promptly dissolved into a puddle of anxiety.

"The core of OCD and the core of all anxiety is uncertainty. In uncertainty there is the potential for danger," Szymanski says. "OCD really has its field day in stress and in transition. Every time people with OCD go through a change, they're stuck with uncertainty. They want to make themselves certain, and they spend all their time replaying what-if scenarios."

Hell, yeah. I spent 3 years of my life wondering if I had AIDS, hepatitis, and every other infection (despite my no-risk behavior and double-digit blood tests). I called the AIDS hotline so often that a counselor finally yelled at me to get off the phone—"You're worried," he said, "but the guy on the other line is dying." I lost whole days of my young adulthood thinking about what I touched, if I had a cut on my hand when I touched it, or if I'd touched my mouth or eyes before washing. Then I'd replay the whole series of events: Did I wash well enough? Am I sure I didn't have a cut? . . .

Fearing the Worst

When I tell Dr. Jenike these details, I don't get the "you freak!" reaction I still brace myself for. "Whatever's the most repugnant to you, that's often what the obsessive thoughts get stuck on," he says. "Like a mother nursing a baby—the mother will think I want to have sex with my baby and be horrified. It seems like OCD is looking for the most repulsive thing to torture people with."

For me, it stopped right there. I never developed the typical hand-washing, repeated-shaving, stove-checking, counting, or touching compulsions. I did not graduate to the level of thinking, "If I do this, then the thing I'm anxious about won't happen." But my girlfriend suspicions and infection worries were plenty bad enough.

Szymanski suggests thinking about it this way: "OCD rituals sound crazy. But find a place within yourself where you experience a negative emotion so powerful that you're willing to do anything—sell your mother—to get away from that emotion. Even if that behavior makes you look crazy to other people. That's the feeling of OCD."

FAST FACT

An estimated 21 to 25 percent of people have borderline OCD; they have obsessions or compulsions meeting some of the diagnostic criteria.

Treating OCD

That feeling finally drove me to a psychopharmacologist, who hit a homer on the first pitch. Prozac wiped out my symptoms within a couple of weeks. I could feel my brain returning to normal.

But most people dealing with OCD require a two-pronged approach of medication (in the form of selective serotonin reuptake inhibitors—SSRIs—like Prozac, Luvox, or Zoloft) and a . . . form of therapy called exposure and response prevention, or ERP. In ERP, a person learns to tolerate repeated exposure to the very cue that triggers the anxiety without acting out the attending ritual. It's administered in stages, with each stage ratcheting up the exposure.

At OCDI, residents work at dealing with their condition for hours and hours each day, all the while agreeing not to carry out the compulsive behaviors that they once used to temporarily neutralize the power of their thoughts. Each ERP is designed to address a particular obsession or compulsion. Compulsive washers will touch toilets and not be allowed to wash. . . .

Repeated exposure to the source of the anxiety, the theory goes, will desensitize a person to it, robbing it of emotional power. In one memorable example, a person with an obsessional fear of stabbing someone was placed in ever greater proximity to knives. Eventually he graduated to standing behind an OCDI staff member for 90 minutes, holding a knife at the ready for a fatal thrust.

No one knows for certain what goes on inside the brain of a person living with OCD, but science is coming much closer to an answer. According to S. Evelyn Stewart, M.D., an assistant professor of psychiatry at Harvard medical school, brain imaging has revealed a biological underpinning for OCD: An over-active loop runs from the brain's decision center (or orbitofrontal cortex) to its movement-governing center (thalamus) and into the basal ganglia, which governs the off switch for thoughts and behaviors.

Benefiting from Mild OCD

In primitive times, obsessive-compulsive traits conferred real advantages to humans. Some elementary fear of pestilence and contamination, the prevention of harm, and the concern about necessities probably set the upwardly mobile cave dweller on the route to success.

Similarly, these traits can give you a leg up in today's workplace, as long as you stop shy of the destructive behaviors that mark the disorder. If you tell a job interviewer that you are obsessed with your work, compulsively neat, and utterly scrupulous, chances are you'll impress him or her with your ability and not your insanity. Double-checking a manuscript can prevent you from leaving a critical "l" out of somebody's public-service award. And I challenge you to find a successful salesman who is not more than a little over the top about closing a deal.

Vladimir Coric, M.D., an associate clinical professor of psychiatry at Yale medical school, runs Yale's OCD research clinic. He believes that "having some obsessive-compulsive traits can be adaptive in some circumstances and contribute to one's success. If you don't worry about the expectations of your boss and the details of your job, you could be fired. It's appropriate to be obsessive and compulsive about important things. If you're able to turn it on and off, it can be a highly adaptive personality trait. If you're not able to turn it off, as with OCD, it can be highly incapacitating."

Preoccupation with detail is like blood pressure: Too much is bad, as is too little.

Men and OCD

Most anxiety disorders tend to skew female. Not so for OCD. Men make up 50 percent of the OCD population and, like me, they tend to develop symptoms earlier in life than women do. And given men's propensity to deny mental disorders, the numbers are probably higher.

But obsessions don't control me anymore. Thanks to chemistry, I've evicted the gnome who forever walked the same path in my mind. The rut he wore has grown over, and my attention no longer sinks into his steps. Still, I've carefully husbanded the obsessive-compulsive traits I like—just enough perfectionism on just the right things, plus a healthy dose of anxiety about my performance and how it is viewed. I rely on them to this day.

The Neuroscience Behind OCD

Wayne Goodman

Wayne Goodman is a pioneer in the research of obsessive-compulsive disorder. He founded the Obsessive Compulsive Disorders Clinic at Yale University and cofounded the Obsessive Compulsive Foundation. He has worked for the National Institute of Mental Health (NIMH) and is currently chair of psychiatry at Mount Sinai School of Medicine. Here, for Psych Central, an online mental health social network run by health professionals, he explains what causes OCD. For at least the past three hundred years, people have described and tried to understand what is now called obsessive-compulsive disorder. Theories have included demon possession, "doubting madness," lack of will and energy, a disrupted psychological development, and the lack of a chemical in the brain called serotonin. However, new technology has provided better ways of scanning a person's conscious brain, allowing researchers to pinpoint areas of the brain that, when damaged or are for some reason overactive, result in obsessive-compulsive behaviors.

SOURCE: Wayne Goodman, "What Causes Obsessive-Compulsive Disorder (OCD)?" Psych Central, December 10, 2006. http://psych central.com. Copyright © 2006 Psych Central. All rights reserved. Reproduced by permission.

A condition resembling OCD has been recognized for more than 300 years. Each stage in the history of OCD has been influenced by the intellectual and scientific climate of the period.

Early theories regarding the cause of a malady similar to OCD stressed the role of distorted religious experience. English writers from the 18th and late 17th centuries attributed intrusive blasphemous images to the work of Satan. Even today, some patients with obsessions of "scrupulosity" still wonder about demonic possession and may seek exorcism.

The French 19th-century accounts of obsessions emphasized the central role of doubt and indecisiveness. In 1837, the French clinician [Jean-Étienne] Esquirol used the term "folie du doute," or the doubting madness, to refer to this cluster of symptoms. Later French writers, including Pierre Janet in 1902, stressed the loss of will and low mental energy as underlying the formation of obsessive-compulsive symptoms.

The Failure of Psychoanalysis

The greater part of the 20th century was dominated by psychoanalytic theories of OCD. According to psychoanalytic theory, obsessions and compulsions reflect maladaptive responses to unresolved conflicts from early stages of psychological development. The symptoms of OCD symbolize the patient's unconscious struggle for control over drives that are unacceptable at a conscious level.

Although often intuitively appealing, psychoanalytic theories of OCD lost favor in the last quarter of the 20th century. Psychoanalysis offers an elaborate metaphor for the mind, but it is not grounded in evidence based on studies of the brain. Psychoanalytic concepts may help explain the content of the patient's obsessions, but they do little to improve understanding of the underlying processes and have not led to reliably effective treatments.

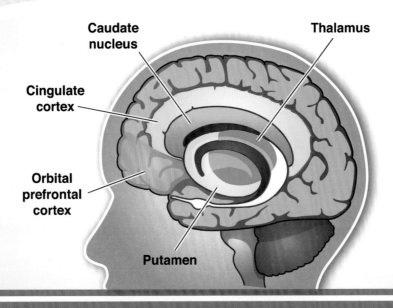

Abnormal Signals in the Obsessive-Compulsive Brain

In patients with OCD, certain functions in the areas of the brain identified below are thought to be associated with obsessive thoughts and impulsive urges.

Caudate nucleus

Thalamus

Cingulate cortex

Orbital prefrontal cortex

Putamen

Taken from: Henrietta L. Leonard, "Obsessive-Compulsive Disorder—the Dana Guide," March 2007.

The psychoanalytic focus on the symbolic meaning of obsessions and compulsions has given way to an emphasis on the form of the symptoms: recurrent, distressing and senseless forced thoughts and actions. The content of symptoms may reveal more about what is most important to or feared by an individual (e.g., moral rectitude, children in harm's way) than why that particular individual developed OCD. Alternatively, the content (e.g., grooming and hoarding) may be related to the activation of fixed action patterns (i.e., innate complex behavioral subroutines) mediated by the brain areas involved in OCD.

The Success of Behavior Therapy

In contrast to psychoanalysis, learning theory models of OCD have gained influence as a result of the success of behavior therapy. Behavior therapy does not concern itself with the psychological origins or meaning of obsessive-compulsive symptoms. The techniques of behavior therapy are built on the theory that obsessions and compulsions are the result of abnormal learned responses and actions. Obsessions are produced when a previously neutral object (e.g., chalk dust) is associated with a stimulus that produces fear (e.g., seeing a classmate have an epileptic fit). Chalk dust becomes connected with a fear of illness even though it played no causative role.

Compulsions (e.g., hand washing) are formed as the individual attempts to reduce the anxiety produced by the learned fearful stimulus (in this case, chalk dust). Avoidance of the object and performance of compulsions reinforces the fear and perpetuates the vicious cycle of OCD. The learned fears also begin to generalize to different stimuli. The fear of contamination with chalk dust may gradually spread to anything that can be found in a classroom, such as textbooks.

> **FAST FACT**
>
> Researchers are close to identifying specific biomarkers linked to OCD, which may be used to identify people with the disorder earlier in life.

The Limitations of Behavior Therapy

Learning theory does not account for all aspects of OCD. It does not adequately explain why some compulsions persist even when they produce, rather than reduce, anxiety. Because compulsions are viewed as a response to obsessions, learning theory does not account for cases in which only compulsions are present. It is also incompatible with obsessive-compulsive symptoms that develop directly as the result of brain injury. These limitations notwithstanding, the effectiveness of a behavior therapy technique referred to as exposure and response prevention has been confirmed in numerous studies.

Limitations of Current Medications

The observation that medications referred to as serotonin reuptake inhibitors (SRIs) are preferentially effective in OCD led researchers to speculate that the brain chemical serotonin might be related to the cause of OCD. The immediate consequence of administering an SRI is to increase the levels of serotonin in the gap between nerve cells called the synapse. However, if this were the only factor involved in the treatment of OCD, one would expect symptoms to improve after the first dose of an SRI. That a response to an SRI takes weeks to develop suggests that the delayed effects of an SRI on brain chemistry are more relevant to OCD than its acute effects.

The effectiveness of SRIs in OCD furnishes important clues about serotonin, but additional research is needed to identify the precise role of this neurochemical in the treatment and cause of OCD.

A Better Look at the Brain

For the first time, advances in technology are allowing researchers to investigate the activity of the waking human brain without causing significant discomfort or risk to the subject. Several of these techniques have been applied to the study of OCD with dramatic results. Lewis R. Baxter Jr. and colleagues of the University of California at Los Angeles and the University of Alabama in Birmingham were the first to use positron-emission tomography (PET) to study OCD.

PET scans produce color-coded images of the brain's metabolic activity. Baxter's study showed that patients with OCD had elevated brain activity in areas of the frontal lobes (particularly the orbital cortex) and the

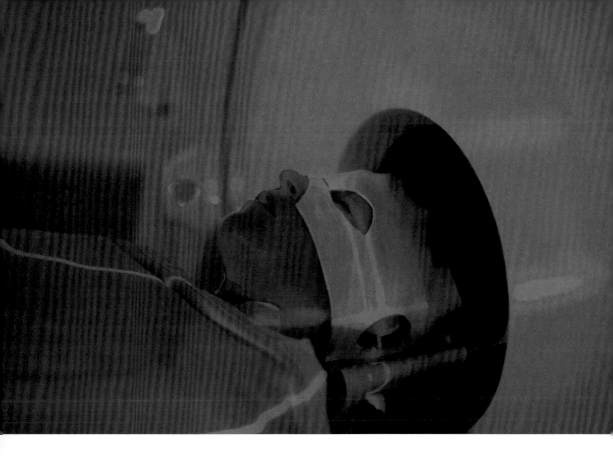

Positron-emission tomography (PET) scans that produce images of the brain are the latest technology to be applied to diagnosing OCD. (Hank Morgan/ Photo Researchers, Inc.)

basal ganglia. Several other groups have since confirmed these findings. Other evidence for a causal role of the basal ganglia in OCD are accidents of nature, such as Sydenham's chorea and von Ecomomo's encephalitis that damage the basal ganglia and produce obsessive-compulsive symptoms.

The Basal Ganglia

The basal ganglia are a group of related brain regions housed deep within the substance of the brain. From an evolutionary standpoint, the basal ganglia are considered primitive structures. Because of their primitive status, until recently, the basal ganglia have been largely ignored in theories of psychiatric illness. Once thought to be a simple relay station in the control of motor behavior, it is now known that the basal ganglia function to integrate information converging from all over the brain.

A Neurological Model

Dr. Judith L. Rapoport of the National Institute of Mental Health has proposed an elegant neurological model of OCD that takes into account both anatomical and clinical evidence. According to this model, the basal ganglia and its connections are turned on inappropriately in OCD. The result is the emergence of self-protective behaviors such as grooming or checking. These primitive behaviors, which are stored as preprogrammed routines in the basal ganglia, unfold uncontrollably outside the reach of brain areas that command reason.

The Classification of OCD

International College of Obsessive Compulsive Spectrum Disorders

Although obsessive-compulsive disorder affects 2 to 3 percent of the population and is one of the world's most debilitating conditions, diagnosis and treatment is difficult. Inadequate classification of OCD within psychological disorders seems to be part of the problem. To analyze this problem and to make recommendations, the Cape Town Consensus Group (CTCG) was formed by the International College of Obsessive Compulsive Spectrum Disorders (ICOCS). The CTCG presented many differences between OCD and anxiety disorders and two possible models of classifying OCD, one including OCD within the group of affective disorders—which includes anxiety and depressive disorders—and the other reclassifying OCD as its own group. The CTCG recommended the latter because the model follows research evidence and should move treatment to become more specific and relevant to the different types of OCD.

SOURCE: International College of Obsessive Compulsive Spectrum Disorders, "Cape Town Consensus Report Published to Drive a 'Revolution' in the Diagnosis and Treatment of Obsessive Compulsive Disorder," www.ICOCS.org, May 29, 2007.

Leading international experts in obsessive compulsive disorder (OCD) have published a new consensus report aimed at providing analysis and guidance to drive improved diagnosis and management of OCD worldwide. Recently presented at The European Congress of Psychiatry in Madrid and published in *CNS Spectrums*, the report has made a number of important recommendations including the removal of OCD from anxiety disorders to create its own category.

"While understanding about OCD has improved greatly in the last 25 years, it still remains significantly under-diagnosed and consequently, patients aren't benefiting from the major advances in treatment," says Professor Joseph Zohar, member of The Cape Town Consensus Group (CTCG) and President of the International College of Obsessive Compulsive Spectrum Disorders (ICOCS). "It became increasingly clear that it was necessary to review the current approach to OCD, since substantial clinical and biological evidence distinguishes it from anxiety disorders. Recognition of this could lead to improvements in the diagnosis and management of this debilitating condition."

> **FAST FACT**
>
> According to the American Psychiatric Association, planning for the new edition of the *Diagnostic and Statistical Manual of Mental Disorders* (*DSM-V*) began in 1999, and the anticipated release date is May 2013.

Prevalence and Diagnosis of OCD

OCD affects between 2–3% of the general population and takes a great toll on sufferers and their friends and families, even if they only experience symptoms for a short time each day. Listed amongst the top 10 most debilitating illnesses by the World Health Organisation (WHO) in terms of loss of income and decreased quality of life, OCD is associated with significant functional disability and economic costs. As well, up to two-thirds of individuals with OCD also suffer from depression at some point during their illness.

Despite this, it takes on average nine years to be diagnosed and 17 years from the time OCD begins for people to obtain appropriate treatment. Further, only a minority of patients fully recover from the disorder.

Evaluating the Classification of OCD

The CTCG was brought together by the ICOCS and an unrestricted educational grant from H. Lundbeck A/S in order to analyse the clinical and scientific evidence that exists in OCD. Current classification systems such as the *Diagnostic and Statistical Manual of Mental Disorders 4th edition (DSM-IV)* and the *International Classification of*

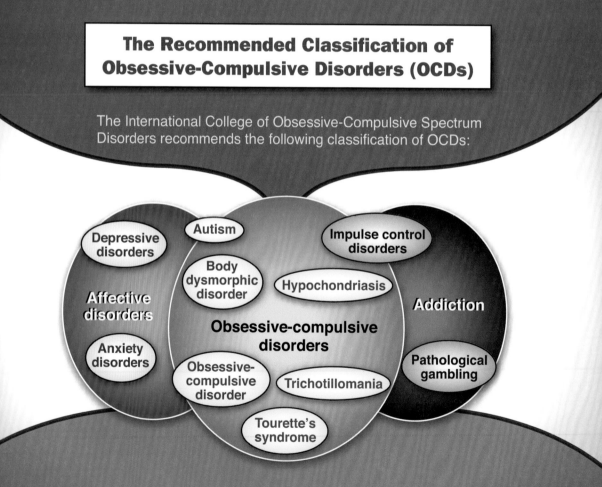

The Recommended Classification of Obsessive-Compulsive Disorders (OCDs)

The International College of Obsessive-Compulsive Spectrum Disorders recommends the following classification of OCDs:

- Depressive disorders
- Autism
- Impulse control disorders
- Affective disorders
- Body dysmorphic disorder
- Hypochondriasis
- Addiction
- Obsessive-compulsive disorders
- Anxiety disorders
- Obsessive-compulsive disorder
- Trichotillomania
- Pathological gambling
- Tourette's syndrome

Taken from: International College of Obsessive Compulsive Spectrum Disorders (ICOCS), "Cape Town Consensus Report Published to Drive a 'Revolution' in the Diagnosis and Treatment of Obsessive Compulsive Disorder," May 29, 2007. www.icocs.org.

Diseases (ICD) differ in the classification of OCD and given the current development of the 5ᵗʰ edition of the *DSM*, the group felt it was important to weigh up the evidence to provide definitive guidance on the most appropriate classification and harmonise current guidelines.

OCD and Anxiety Disorders Are Different

The CTCG . . . analysis highlighted a number of areas that separate OCD from anxiety disorders including:

- Its potential onset during puberty whereas other anxiety disorders have a later age of onset
- Its equal prevalence amongst men and women as opposed to depressive and anxiety disorders which are more common in women
- The difference in brain circuitry that mediates OCD compared to that involved in fear, stress-related or mood disorders
- Its uniquely specific response to serotonin reuptake inhibitors, while noradrenergic medications (effective in anxiety and mood) are largely ineffective
- The increasing evidence for treatment augmentation with second-generation antipsychotics, suggesting an important role of dopamine in OCD (which is not seen in other anxiety disorders)
- Its lack of treatment response to benzodiazepines which can be effective in anxiety disorders

Current Treatment of OCD

There are two treatments that have been proven to be effective against OCD. They include cognitive behaviour therapy (CBT) and medication, primarily through selective serotonin reuptake inhibitors (SSRIs). SSRIs have proven to be beneficial as it appears that potent effects on brain serotonin are necessary to produce improvement in OCD. The CTCG also highlights the growing

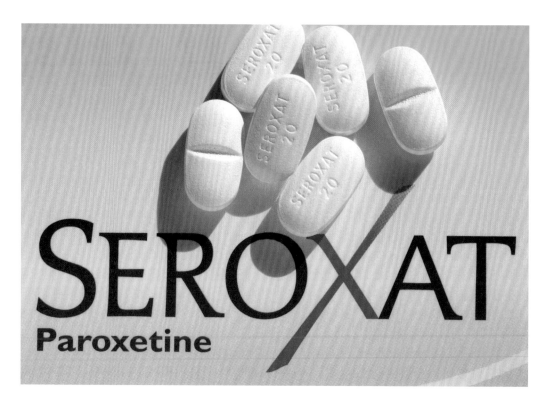

SEROXAT
Paroxetine

Selective serotonin reuptake inhibitors (SSRIs), found in medications such as this one, have proved effective in treating OCD. (Saturn Stills/ Photo Researchers, Inc.)

evidence of the role of dopamine in OCD, pointing to the potential for the use of second generation antipsychotics within the treatment pathway. . . .

A Future Definition of OCD?

Two potential methods [have been] put forth by the CTCG to categorise OCD. [The first] places OCD within a broad spectrum of affective spectrum disorders, whereas [the second] presents OCD as a group of disorders lying midway between affective disorders and addiction disorders.

Both recommendations recognise that there are actually a range of OCD subtypes which are currently classified within the umbrella of 'OCD'. These subtypes can be classified based on clinical symptoms (i.e. OCD combined with tics or hoarding), by treatment response and family studies.

Although reclassifying OCD as a distinct group of disorders may complicate the diagnostic process and fragment the concept of anxiety, the CTCG strongly recommends this approach as the proposed classification is a better fit with clinical evidence and may improve the management of OCD by moving towards treatment tailored to specific subtypes of OCD.

"Recognising the complex and varied presentation of OCD will enable the tailoring of treatment according to the specific profile of the individual patient and therefore could contribute to better treatment outcomes," says Naomi Fineberg, Consultant Psychiatrist and Honorary Senior Lecturer, Imperial College London and University of Hertfordshire. "OCD is a chronic condition requiring long-term treatment and if we can move towards management of OCD in this way we stand a much better chance of treatment success and relapse prevention to enable patients to better function in their everyday lives."

Advances in the Treatment of OCD

Society for Neuroscience

The Society for Neuroscience, a nonprofit organization of doctors and scientists who study the brain and nervous system, publishes *Brain Briefings*, a monthly newsletter written for the general public. *Brain Briefings*: "Obsessive-Compulsive Disorder" discusses the best current treatments for OCD, which include behavioral therapy, medications, or a combination of behavioral therapy and medication. Cutting-edge treatments, including deep brain stimulation and transcranial magnetic stimulation, are also discussed.

The scrubbing continues. And continues. And continues. Your breakfast remains barely touched while you repeatedly detour to the sink to scour your hands, 15 times so far.

Some say you're quirky, but it's much more than that. Approximately 3.3 million American adults suffer from obsessive-compulsive disorder, or OCD, a serious and

SOURCE: *Brain Briefings,* "Obsessive-Compulsive Disorder," Summer 2006. Copyright © 2006 Society for Neuroscience. Reproduced by permission.

very real anxiety disorder that is characterized by irrational, recurring thoughts, such as an excessive concern with germs and dirt or a fixation on order. These obsessional thoughts may lead people with OCD to constantly repeat behaviors, like hand-washing or arranging objects symmetrically, to help ease their anxiety and keep the obsessive thoughts at bay. The process can sideline daily life activities, relationships, and careers, but does little to stop the obsessions from resurfacing.

Deep brain stimulation is shown in this computer artwork. Initially developed to relieve symptoms in Parkinson's disease patients, it is now being used to treat OCD. (Tim Vernon, LTH NHS Trust/Photo Researchers, Inc.)

Increased Research

Scientists, however, are now finding better ways to break OCD's hold. Increasing research is pushing forward the development of new treatments, including a possible medication that may help mute the intrusive thoughts of people with OCD, as well as stimulation techniques that alter brain activity to relieve symptoms. The advances are leading to:

- A clearer understanding of the mechanisms that underlie fear and OCD.
- Additional treatment options that target diverse brain mechanisms to aid those with hard-to-treat forms of OCD.

Behavioral Therapy

One component of OCD treatment centers on behavioral techniques that help people regain control over their irrational behavior. People who continuously wash their hands in fear of germs may be urged to touch an object thought to be dirty and then encouraged to refuse to wash for several hours. The therapy, when properly applied, is highly effective, but the number of skilled practitioners is limited.

Medication

Drugs used for depression that alter certain brain chemicals and decrease anxiety also can successfully help treat OCD. Drugs typically used to treat OCD act on cells in the brain that affect levels of the brain chemical serotonin, which different parts of the brain linked to OCD use to communicate with each other. Serotonin is known to affect mood and anxiety levels. But the medications don't aid everyone.

Combinations of Medications and Therapy

Scientists continue to pursue research to find treatment strategies for those who don't respond to these medications. These strategies include new medications, combinations of currently used drugs with those used to treat other mental disorders, and behavior therapy paired with medication.

D-Cycloserine

Recently, researchers have identified new techniques that could increase the number of treatments for OCD and possibly help a wider range of people. Included is the compound D-cycloserine. First, animal research helped scientists determine that D-cycloserine boosts activity of a brain cell component termed the NMDA receptor, which is implicated in general learning. The compound also enhanced the ability of rats to overcome their fears. When combined in low doses with the kind of behavioral therapy described above, it helps people conquer their fears.

Deep Brain Stimulation

Other strategies, like deep brain stimulation, also may translate soon into new treatments for OCD. This technique, comprised of a brain implant that delivers electrical pulses to alter brain activity, already has helped many patients with tremors and the movement disorder Parkinson's disease achieve greater movement control. Small studies recently found evidence that deep brain stimulation in certain brain areas also can relieve symptoms of OCD. Larger studies of the technique are in progress.

Transcranial Magnetic Stimulation

Another stimulation technique, transcranial magnetic stimulation, also holds promise. Instead of a brain implant, the technique relies on an electromagnetic coil held against the patient's scalp that emits powerful magnetic

> **FAST FACT**
>
> Genetics research will assist doctors in deciding which treatment to use with a specific case of OCD. The effectiveness of a treatment may depend on whether it is the right treatment for the genetic variation that is associated with the particular case of OCD.

Transcranial Magnetic Stimulation

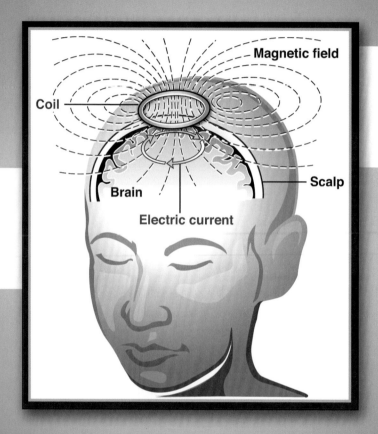

Taken from: Society for Neuroscience, *Brain Briefings:* "Obsessive-Compulsive Disorder," Summer 2006.

pulses to alter brain activity. Following positive results in a small study, researchers have begun a larger study that will include 50 people with OCD.

As advances continue, more people plagued by OCD soon may be able to put down the hand soap and regain control of their lives.

CHAPTER 2

Issues and Controversies Concerning OCD

Some Cases of OCD Are Triggered by Strep Throat Infections

National Institute of Mental Health, Pediatric Developmental Neuroscience Branch

The National Institute of Mental Health (NIMH) is part of the National Institutes of Health (NIH), a component of the U.S. Department of Health and Human Services. The NIMH comprises many specialized branches, including the Pediatric Developmental Neuroscience Branch, which has conducted patient studies on pediatric autoimmune neuropsychiatric disorders associated with streptococcal infections (PANDAS). This article explains the NIH's current theory of PANDAS and provides general information and answers to frequently asked questions about PANDAS, covering topics such as how PANDAS are diagnosed, what the symptoms may be, and what treatments exist.

Photo on previous page. Many children who contract strep throat display symptoms of pediatric autoimmune neuropsychiatric disorders (PANDAS). (**Photo Researchers, Inc.**)

PANDAS, is an abbreviation for Pediatric Autoimmune Neuropsychiatric Disorders Associated with Streptococcal Infections. The term is used to describe a subset of children who have Obsessive Compulsive Disorder (OCD) and/or tic disorders such as Tourette's Syndrome, and in whom symptoms worsen following strep infections such as "Strep throat" and Scarlet Fever.

SOURCE: National Institute of Mental Health, *PANDAS*, February 24, 2009. http://intramural.nimh/nih.gov/pdn/web.htm.

The children usually have dramatic, "overnight" onset of symptoms, including motor or vocal tics, obsessions, and/or compulsions. In addition to these symptoms, children may also become moody, irritable or show concerns about separating from parents or loved ones. This abrupt onset is generally preceeded by a Strep throat infection.

What is the mechanism behind this phenomenon? At present, it is unknown but researchers at the NIMH are pursuing a theory that the mechanism is similar to that of Rheumatic Fever, an autoimmune disorder triggered by strep throat infections. In every bacterial infection, the body produces antibodies against the invading bacteria, and the antibodies help eliminate the bacteria from the body. However in Rheumatic Fever, the antibodies mistakenly recognize and "attack" the heart valves, joints, and/or certain parts of the brain. This phenomenon is called "molecular mimicry," which means that proteins on the cell wall of the strep bacteria are similar in some way to the proteins of the heart valve, joints, or brain. Because the antibodies set off an immune reaction which damages those tissues, the child with Rheumatic Fever can get heart disease . . . arthritis, and/or abnormal movements known as Sydenham's Chorea or St. Vitus Dance.

In PANDAS, it is believed that something very similar to Sydenham's Chorea occurs. One part of the brain that is affected in PANDAS is the Basal Ganglia, which is believed to be responsible for movement and behavior. Thus, the antibodies interact with the brain to cause tics and/or OCD, instead of Sydenham's Chorea.

Frequently Asked Questions

Q. *Is there a test for PANDAS?*
A. No. The diagnosis of PANDAS is a clinical diagnosis, which means that there are no lab tests that can diagnose PANDAS. Instead clinicians use 5 diagnostic

criteria for the diagnosis of PANDAS (see below). At the present time the clinical features of the illness are the only means of determining whether or not a child might have PANDAS.

Q. *What are the diagnostic criteria for PANDAS?*
A. They are:
1. Presence of Obsessive-compulsive disorder and/or a tic disorder
2. Pediatric onset of symptoms (age 3 years to puberty)
3. Episodic course of symptom severity
4. Association with group A Beta-hemolytic streptococcal infection (a positive throat culture for strep, or history of Scarlet Fever.)
5. Association with neurological abnormalities (motoric hyperactivity, or adventitious movements, such as choreiform movements)

Q. *What is an episodic course of symptoms?*
A. Children with PANDAS seem to have dramatic ups and downs in their OCD and/or tic severity. Tics or OCD which are almost always present at a relatively consistent level do not represent an episodic course. Many kids with OCD or tics have good days and bad days, or even good weeks and bad weeks. However, patients with PANDAS have a very sudden onset or worsening of their symptoms, followed by a slow, gradual improvement. If they get another strep infection, their symptoms suddenly worsen again. The increased symptom severity usually persists for at least several weeks, but may last for several months or longer. The tics or OCD then seem to gradually fade away, and the children often enjoy a few weeks or several months without problems. When they have another strep throat infection the tics or OCD return just as suddenly and dramatically as they did previously.

Q. *Are there any other symptoms associated with PANDAS episodes?*

A. Yes. Children with PANDAS often experience one or more of the following symptoms in conjunction with their OCD and/or tics:

1. ADHD symptoms (hyperactivity, inattention, fidgety)
2. Separation anxiety (Child is "clingy" and has difficulty separating from his/her caregivers. For example, the child may not want to be in a different room in the house from his/her parents.)

School-Related Symptoms or Behaviors Indicative of Obsessive-Compulsive Disorder

- Unproductive time retracing the same word or touching the same objects over and over
- Erasing sentences or problems repeatedly
- Counting and recounting objects, or arranging and rearranging objects on their desk
- Frequent trips to the bathroom
- Poor concentration
- School avoidance
- Anxiety or depressed mood

Taken from: Minnesota Association for Children's Mental Health, St. Paul, Minnesota. www.macmh.org.

3. Mood changes (irritability, sadness, emotional lability)
4. Sleep disturbance
5. Night-time bed wetting and/or day-time urinary frequency
6. Fine/gross motor changes (e.g. changes in handwriting)
7. Joint pains

Q. *My child has had strep throat before, and he has tics and/or OCD. Does that mean he has PANDAS?*
A. No. Many children have OCD and/or tics, and almost all school aged children get strep throat at some point in their lives. In fact, the average grade-school student will have 2–3 strep throat infections each year. PANDAS is considered when there is a very close relationship between the abrupt onset or worsening of OCD and/or tics, and a preceding strep infection. If strep is found in conjunction with two or three episodes of OCD/tics, then it may be that the child has PANDAS.

Q. *Could an adult have PANDAS?*
A. No. By definition, PANDAS is a pediatric disorder. It is possible that adolescents and adults may have immune mediated OCD, but this is not known. The research studies at the NIMH are restricted to children.

Q. *My child has PANDAS. Should he have his tonsils removed?*
A. The NIH does not recommend tonsillectomies for children with PANDAS, as there is no evidence that they are helpful. If a tonsillectomy is recommended because of frequent episodes of tonsillitis, it would be useful to discuss the pros and cons of the procedure with your child's doctor, because of the role that the tonsils play in fighting strep infections.

Q. *What exactly is an anti-streptococcal antibody titer?*
A. The anti-streptococcal antibody titer [the concentration or strength of a substance] determines whether

there is immunologic evidence of a previous strep infection. Two different strep tests are commercially available: the antistrepolysin O (ASO) titer, which rises 3–6 weeks after a strep infection, and the antistreptococcal DNAase B (AntiDNAse-B) titer, which rises 6–8 weeks after a strep infection.

Shown here is a diagnostic test used to detect streptococcal pharyngitis. A strep throat test is one of five diagnostic criteria for PANDAS. **(Philippe Garo/Photo Researchers, Inc.)**

Q. What does an elevated anti-streptococcal antibody titer mean? Is this bad for my child?
A. An elevated anti-strep titer (such as ASO or Anti-DNAse-B) means the child has had a strep infection sometime within the past few months, and his body created antibodies to fight the strep bacteria. Some children create lots of antibodies and have very high titers (up to 2,000), while others have more modest elevations. The height of the titer elevation doesn't matter. Further, elevated titers are not a bad thing. They are measuring a normal, healthy response—the production of antibodies

to fight off an infection. The antibodies stay in the body for some time after the infection is gone, but the amount of time that the antibodies persist varies greatly between different individuals. Some children have "positive" antibody titers for many months after a single infection.

Q. *When is a strep titer considered to be abnormal, or "elevated"?*
A. The lab at NIH considers strep titers between 0–400 to be normal. Other labs set the upper limit at 150 or 200. Since each lab measures titers in different ways, it is important to know the range used by the laboratory where the test was done—just ask where they draw the line between negative or positive titers.

It is important to note that some grade-school aged children have chronically "elevated" titers. These may actually be in the normal range for that child, as there is a lot of individual variability in titer values. Because of this variability, doctors will often draw a titer when the child is sick, or shortly thereafter, and then draw another titer several weeks later to see if the titer is "rising"—if so, this is strong evidence that the illness was due to strep. (Of course, a less expensive way to make this determination is to take a throat culture at the time that the child is ill.)

Q. *Should an elevated strep titer be treated with antibiotics?*
A. No. Elevated titers indicate that a patient has had a past strep exposure but the titers cannot tell you precisely when the strep infection occurred. Children may have "positive" titers for many months after one infection. Since these elevated titers are merely a marker of a prior infection and not proof of an ongoing infection it is not appropriate to give antibiotics for elevated titers.

FAST FACT

A study in the July 2005 issue of *Pediatrics* suggests that strep infections in young children may double the risk for sudden onset of OCD, Tourette's syndrome, or tic disorder within a three-month period following the infection.

Antibiotics are recommended only when a child has a positive rapid strep test or positive strep throat culture.

Q. *What are the treatment options for children with PAN-DAS?*
A. The treatments for children with PANDAS are the same as if they had other types of OCD or tic disorders. Children with OCD, regardless of whether or not their illness is strep triggered, benefit from cognitive behavioral therapy and/or anti-obsessional medications. A recent study showed that the combination of an SSRI medication (such as fluoxetine) and cognitive behavioral therapy was the best treatment for OCD, and that medication alone or cognitive behavioral therapy alone were better than no treatment, or use of a placebo (sugar pill). It often takes time for these treatments to work, so the sooner therapy is started, the better it is for the child.

Children with strep triggered tics should be helped by the same tic medications that doctors use to treat other tic disorders. Your child's primary physician can help you decide which type of specialist your child may need to see to receive these treatments.

Q. *Can penicillin be used to treat PANDAS or prevent future PANDAS symptom exacerbations?*
A. Penicillin and other antibiotics kill streptococcus and other types of bacteria. The antibiotics treat the sore throat or pharyngitis caused by the strep by getting rid of the bacteria. However, in PANDAS, it appears that antibodies produced by the body in response to the strep infection are the cause of the problem, not the bacteria themselves. Therefore one could not expect antibiotics such as penicillin to treat the symptoms of PANDAS. Researchers at the NIMH have been investigating the use of antibiotics as a form of prophylaxis or prevention of future problems. At this time, however, there isn't enough evidence to recommend the long-term use of antibiotics.

Q. *What about treating PANDAS with plasma exchange or immunoglobulin (IVIG)?*

A. The results of a controlled trial of plasma exchange (also known as plasmapheresis) and immunoglobulin (IVIG) for the treatment of children in the PANDAS subgroup was published in *The Lancet*, Vol. 354, October 2, 1999. All of the children participating in the study had clear evidence of a strep infection as the trigger of their OCD and tics, and all were severely ill at the time of treatment. The study showed that plasma exchange and IVIG were both effective for the treatment of severe, strep triggered OCD and tics, and that there were persistent benefits of the interventions. However, there were a number of side-effects associated with the treatments, including nausea, vomiting, headaches and dizziness. In addition, there is a risk of infection with any invasive procedure, such as these. Thus, the treatments should be reserved for severely ill patients, and administered by a qualified team of health care professionals. The NIH is not currently conducting any trials with immunomodulatory therapies, and so is not able to offer either of the treatments.

Of note, a separate study was conducted to evaluate the effectiveness of plasma exchange in the treatment of chronic OCD. None of those children benefited, suggesting that plasma exchange or IVIG is not helpful for children who do not have strep triggered OCD or tics.

OCD Is Rarely, If Ever, Triggered by Strep Throat Infections

Walter A. Brown

Walter A. Brown is clinical professor of psychiatry at Brown University Medical School in Providence, Rhode Island, and Tufts University School of Medicine in Boston. He writes here for *Psychiatric Times,* a periodical focused on psychiatric news. In 1998 researchers coined the term PANDAS (pediatric autoimmune neuropsychiatric disorders associated with streptococcal infection). In short, it describes cases where children develop obsessive-compulsive disorder following a strep throat infection. Brown contends that parents have been happy to embrace this idea because it brought the hope of recovering from OCD with antibiotics. Many doctors who see children with possible PANDAS have been treating them with antibiotics, as well as plasma exchange and immunoglobulin therapy for antibody deficiency. Brown notes that despite the acceptance of PANDAS by parents, doctors, textbooks, and the media, the actual existence of PANDAS has not yet been established with reliable, large population studies.

At first glance, PANDAS (Pediatric Autoimmune Neuropsychiatric Disorders Associated with Streptococcal infection) has little in common with the cuddly bear that roams the bamboo forests of southwest China. But, in fact, they share 2 important features: both are rare and both are threatened with extinction. A handful of ongoing PANDAS studies challenge its survival, and the outcomes of those studies will have an impact on how neurologists and other physicians evaluate and treat children with obsessive-compulsive symptoms and tics.

The idea that streptococcal infections can precipitate neuropsychiatric disorders in children, including obsessive-compulsive symptoms and tics, has surfaced intermittently for more than 100 years. It was not until 1998 that this notion was fully articulated. In that year, Susan E. Swedo, MD, and her colleagues published their findings on 50 such cases, provided criteria for making the diagnosis, and gave the syndrome the name and acronym that has stuck. . . .

As far back as the late 19th century, William Osler (1849–1919) noted "a certain perseverativeness of behavior" in children with Sydenham chorea [a neurological disorder associated with strep infections]. Others made similar observations. Swedo and colleagues found a high prevalence of OCD symptoms. Swedo also carried out longitudinal studies of children with OCD. She found that a subgroup of such children had a pattern of abrupt onset of OCD, an episodic course, and exacerbations that often preceded group A b-hemolytic streptococcal (GABHS) infections.

A Unique Subgroup?

Swedo and colleagues suggested that these children represent a unique subgroup defined by: (1) OCD and/or a tic disorder; (2) onset between age 3 and the beginning of puberty; (3) episodic course characterized by abrupt

In the late nineteenth century Canadian physician William Osler noted that children with Sydenham chorea had "a certain perseverativeness of behavior" that is now associated with PANDAS. **(Hulton Archive/Getty Images)**

onset of symptoms or dramatic symptom exacerbations; (4) temporal association with GABHS infection; and (5) neurologic abnormalities during symptom exacerbations. They postulated that as in Sydenham chorea, GABHS infections, through a process of molecular mimicry, trigger in susceptible children an autoimmune response targeted to neurons. The presence in some children with PANDAS of the same antineuronal antibodies found in Sydenham chorea provided support for this hypothesis. Swedo points out that children with PANDAS, unlike those with Sydenham chorea, don't get frank chorea or the cardiac and other manifestations of rheumatic fever. She suggests that the causative agent may be the same in both conditions but that the "dose" is lower in PANDAS.

An Appealing Explanation

The PANDAS concept captivated pediatricians and child psychiatrists. It provided an explanation for a condition that heretofore seemed to arise out of nowhere; the proposed etiology and pathophysiology made sense, not only on its own merits but also because it followed the established and widely accepted model of Sydenham chorea. Most compelling of all, it promised a simple, effective, and safe treatment.

Tics can be suppressed, but the drugs commonly used to treat them (antipsychotics and others) are beset with side effects. Also, the mainstays of OCD treatment, selective serotonin reupake inhibitor antidepressants and cognitive behavioral therapy, bring meaningful improvement to far fewer than half of those treated. The idea that these conditions would clear up with a course of antibiotics had tremendous appeal not only to the clinicians struggling to help these kids but, not surprisingly, to their parents as well.

> **FAST FACT**
>
> The incidence of PANDAS peaks at ages five to twelve years—the same ages at which strep infections peak.

Despite the paucity of data in support of it and the uncertainty about its prevalence, the PANDAS concept took hold. Current pediatric and psychiatric textbooks refer to it as an established, albeit possibly rare, phenomenon. Although a rash of studies call the concept into question, and although many clinicians have never seen PANDAS, few are ready to abandon the idea of it.

Joseph Friedman, MD, chief of neurology at Memorial Hospital of Rhode Island, doesn't treat kids and has never seen PANDAS, but as is typical of many in the field, he has a generous approach to the concept. It hasn't been proved, Friedman said, and it's probably overdiagnosed, but PANDAS makes sense: "I'm willing to believe it exists."

The concept of PANDAS has not been confined to medical dialogue. In January 2004, *USA Today* carried an article on OCD in children. PANDAS, according to this article, accounts for 1 in 10 cases of OCD in children, and if treated promptly with antibiotics, "symptoms can in many cases disappear in days."

The Clinical Value

If only this claim were so. The clinical value of PANDAS rests on the promise of antibiotic treatment, and here the results of controlled trials have been, at best, inconclusive. Penicillin prophylaxis [used for prevention] in one controlled study didn't prevent exacerbations of tics and OCD, but it didn't prevent streptococcal pharyngitis either. Swedo and her colleagues have recently [2005] completed a penicillin prophylaxis study, as yet unpublished, which, she said, shows that the antibiotic does relieve PANDAS symptoms. For now, the most compelling case for the value of antibiotic treatment comes from an uncontrolled study of 12 kids who met PANDAS criteria and improved with antibiotics, and the testimonials of clinicians and investigators who have seen tics and OCD symptoms disappear in individual children treated with antibiotics. But clinical observations of this sort, convincing as they might appear, mislead at least as often as they point to useful information. Clinicians who have given antibiotics to children who meet PANDAS criteria have not been uniformly impressed.

Many Doctors Reluctant to Dismiss PANDAS

Henry Sachs, MD, a child psychiatrist at Bradley Hospital in East Providence, RI, believes that PANDAS exists and when he sees a child with acute onset of tics or OCD, he gets a throat culture and checks antistreptolysin O (ASO) and anti-DNase B titers [the concentration or strength of a substance]. He has seen elevated ASO and anti-DNase titers in association with exacerbations of tics but points out that since he usually doesn't have a baseline, he doesn't know whether these elevations represent a recent increase in titers and that it's the change in titers that reliably indicates recent infection.

Nevertheless, when these lab tests raise the possibility of recent or current streptococcal infection, he prescribes antibiotics. He admitted, though, "I haven't seen much benefit from them." Despite his skepticism, Sachs, like many clinicians, is reluctant to abandon the promise of antibiotic treatment. He said that the next time he comes across a child with an acute onset of tics or OCD and signs of streptococcal infection, he will again treat with antibiotics but "without a great expectation that it will help."

Neurologists More Skeptical

Neurologists have, in general, been more critical of the PANDAS concept than pediatricians and child psychiatrists. Part of the reason may be that neurologists see more children with tics than with OCD. Typical OCD has a gradual onset and a stable course and is quite resistant to treatment. An acute onset or exacerbation of OCD, as described in kids with PANDAS, is different from the usual OCD course. But the course of PANDAS tics is not all that different from that of ordinary tics. As Roger Kurlan, MD, a neurologist at the University of Rochester School of Medicine, points out, tics have a waxing and waning course and get worse with any sort of stress, including that of illness. That tics worsen in the context of streptococcal infection doesn't necessarily mean that the pathogen has a specific etiologic [causative] role. . . .

No Professional Consensus

In part because so little data and, as yet, no definitive studies exist about PANDAS, almost everything about the concept is a matter of controversy. Critics and advocates of PANDAS draw different conclusions from the same data. The 1999 *Lancet* paper describing the results of immunomodulatory therapy is a case in point. Twenty-nine children with PANDAS were treated with either plasmapheresis or intravenous immunoglobulin (IVIG). The IVIG, but not the plasmapheresis, was placebo-controlled.

The children showed dramatic improvement in tic and OCD symptoms. According to Swedo, who was one of the study investigators, improvement was far greater than that achieved with standard treatments.

To advocates of the PANDAS concept, this study provided important proof of the autoimmune pathophysiology. But . . . other skeptics call attention to flaws in the study's design, including the highly selected patient population, concurrent use of psychotropic drugs, and the limited controls. They think that this study may prove little more than that the symptoms in these kids fluctuate over time and are highly placebo-responsive.

PANDAS Is Rare

A recent study by Eliana Perrin, MD, and her colleagues seemed to deal a near-fatal blow to PANDAS as a diagnosis. Perrin is an assistant professor of pediatrics at the University of North Carolina, Chapel Hill, School of Medicine. They observed 814 children in a large pediatric practice. Half developed GABHS infections, a quarter developed viral illnesses, and a quarter remained well. No children developed full-blown PANDAS, and the children with streptococcal infections were no more likely to develop OCD symptoms or tics than those who remained well or had presumed viral illnesses. Swedo, one of the report's authors, is undeterred by these results. She explained that PANDAS is rare—she estimates that it accounts for fewer than 5% of children with OCD and tics—and she thinks that a larger sample may be required to find it.

That PANDAS is rare does seem to be one point on which both researchers and clinicians agree. In one pediatric practice, among 4000 children with streptococcal infection seen over a 3-year period, only 12 had PANDAS. Alison Days, MD, a pediatrician and medical director of Texas Tech's Child Wellness Center in El Paso, learned about PANDAS during her pediatrics residency. "My colleagues have seen 2 kids who may have had PANDAS,"

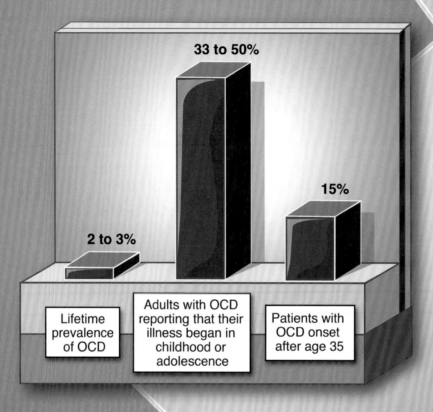

The Prevalence of OCD Throughout the Life Span

33 to 50%

15%

2 to 3%

Lifetime prevalence of OCD

Adults with OCD reporting that their illness began in childhood or adolescence

Patients with OCD onset after age 35

Taken from: Henrietta L. Leonard, "Obsessive-Compulsive Disorder—the Dana Guide," March 2007.

she said, "but I haven't seen any, and I see loads of kids with strep. I guess I believe in it but it's so rare I don't think of it very often."

More Study Results Forthcoming

Several large-scale prospective studies of PANDAS funded by the NIH [National Institutes of Health] are now under way. They should help resolve the controversy both about whether PANDAS is real—whether a subgroup of kids with OCD and tics have their symptoms precipitated by GABHS—and whether prophylactic penicillin treatment of these children can prevent relapses.

The Answer Is Important

The clinical stakes are high. If PANDAS proves as resilient as its bamboo-chewing namesake, clinicians will have a firm rationale for checking throat cultures and titers in children with abrupt OCD and tic onset. More important, a subgroup of children who suffer with these symptoms will have the promise of rapid symptom relief with antibiotics. Conversely, if these studies do not support PANDAS, clinicians will have little justification for diagnostic tests for streptococcal infection.

Inconclusive as the existing data are, a PANDAS "signal" does come through. Ongoing prospective studies may show PANDAS to be so rare that it is clinically insignificant. However rare it might be, says Swedo, PANDAS provides a window into the "neurocircuitry of OCD and tics," and, she continued, "we never thought of it as anything else."

Having Obsessive Bad Thoughts Is a Form of OCD

Steve Kissing

Steve Kissing is a contributing editor and the award-winning writer of the "Odd Man Out" column in *Cincinnati* magazine. In 2003 he published his memoir, *Running from the Devil: A Memoir of a Boy Possessed*. In this article he writes about obsessive bad thoughts (OBT), a type of OCD in which its victims cannot stop thinking about doing something violent or inappropriate but never act on the thoughts. OBT can take on many forms, such as the urge to shout out inappropriate comments or the urge to throw a dog out of a car window. Many sufferers struggle silently, terrified that they will lose control and act on their thoughts. Simply trying to ignore the thoughts only makes them worse. Some people are helped by counseling and some by exposure and response prevention therapy.

Had you met me, or even just walked past me, anytime around 1989, there's a good chance that I thought seriously about jabbing a pencil into your eye. And not a stubby pencil with chew marks but

SOURCE: Steve Kissing, "Trouble in Mind: It's OK to Laugh at Obsessive Bad Thoughts—Until Someone Gets an Eye Poked Out," *Cincinnati*, vol. 39, March 2006, pp. 48, 50–53. Copyright © 2006 Emmis Publishing, L.P. Reproduced by permission.

a fresh No. 2, carefully sharpened. . . . I obsessed over this spear-in-the-eye thought countless times and worried about actually doing it. Even though I didn't want to do it. Even though I felt horrible for even thinking such a bad thought. Even though, to this day, I nearly faint whenever I see someone adjust a contact lens.

Nuts, huh? Of course it's wacko, but I'm not alone. While there may not be others walking in your midst who want to cut your cornea, there are plenty of people who obsess over other bad thoughts. This condition, Obsessive Bad Thoughts (OBT), is a form of Obsessive Compulsive Disorder (OCD). It's estimated that about 3.3 million Americans are compelled to repeat useless rituals, including obsessing over bad thoughts.

Obsessive Bad Thoughts Take Many Forms

In his book *The Imp of the Mind: Exploring the Silent Epidemic of Obsessive Bad Thoughts*, Lee Baer, Ph.D., describes the many forms these thoughts can take. Some OBT sufferers obsess about violent things, like pouring hot coffee over someone's head. Some obsess over sexual thoughts, like French kissing a cousin during Thanksgiving dinner. Others obsess over losing control in public and doing something they shouldn't, like licking the sneeze shield on the salad bar at [a restaurant].

Rest assured, I've never poked anyone in the eye with a pencil. Or a pen. Or any other sharp object. Heck, I can't even remember the last time I sharpened a pencil. But the weird thing is, there was a time I really *thought* I would do it.

Thoughts That Are Impossible to Ignore

First I tried to master my bad thoughts by ignoring them. To avoid temptation, I boycotted places where pencils are found in abundance: accounting firms, golf courses, S.A.T. testing centers, etc. Of course, the more you try

Symptoms of Pure Obsessional OCD, or Obsessional Bad Thoughts

- Intrusive thoughts or mental images of killing one's parent or child

- Recurrent fear of molesting a child

- Repeatedly worrying that one did or will physically assault another person or run over a pedestrian while driving a car

- Repetitive thoughts that one has said or written something inappropriate, such as swearing at an employer or writing hate-filled letters to a friend

- Intrusive thoughts or mental images that one considers to be sacrilegious or blasphemous, such as wanting to worship Satan or have sex with Christ

Taken from: OCD Center of Los Angeles, "Pure Obsessional OCD ('Pure O')—Symptoms and Treatment," www.ocdla.com/obsessionalOCD.html.

not to think about something, the more you think about it. There's a classic psychology experiment in which a group of people are shown a photo of a white bear and then told not to think about it. Another group is shown the same photo but they're free to think about it, if they so choose. Does it surprise you that the group that was told not to think about the bear did little else but think about it? It's much like when young boys are told not to stare at a woman's boobs.

Thinking about a white bear—or a boob, for that matter—especially (in either case) a cute, cuddly one—

seems relatively benign. But shoving pencils into people's eyes, well, that's a different story. As is obsessing over the thought that you might pour an extra-hot, one-and-a-half pump mocha over someone's head. Or that you might drop your pants in public and shout "Free love!"

Jumping Off of a Bridge

OBT manifestations are as nuanced as the people who struggle with them. For instance, take an acquaintance of mine who I'll call Paul. (I've changed the names of the OBT sufferers I interviewed out of respect for their privacy.) Paul is a successful young businessman who generally loves life; as the joke goes, he'd kill himself before he'd ever attempt suicide. But the moment he steps on a bridge or elevated pedestrian walkway, he is seized by the thought of leaping over the railing. Sometimes it helps if he holds on to something or someone; other times, he'd rather be left alone and not make physical contact with anything or anyone.

Paul's not afraid of heights and has no problems with flying, tall buildings, or riding roller coasters. But whenever he finds himself walking over a bridge, he struggles to stay focused. Some bridges can be avoided, of course, but many can't—unless you're willing to swim across rivers or negotiate the hazards of a rail-yard, which isn't easy to do when you're wearing a pinstriped suit and toting a leather brief-case. After about a year of sweating over these thoughts, Paul sought counseling from a licensed therapist. Within months his bad thoughts faded. "I can now cross a bridge and not worry about bungee jumping without the bungee cord," he says.

> **FAST FACT**
>
> One in fifty adults has OCD, and 10 to 20 percent of them have obsessive sexual thoughts.

Stomping on the Dog

Another friend, call her Jenny, fights off repeated thoughts about tossing Webster, the dog she adopted . . . out her car window while driving on I-75. OK, let's not cast stones: We've *all* fantasized about shoving an irritating passenger out the window. Most of us just get a quick little boost as we envision our annoying mother-in-law, motor-mouth colleague, or ungrateful spouse bouncing off the pavement. We smile and then quickly move on, no worries, no guilt. We don't think about it—incessantly—until we're so full of guilt we worry when we even think about thinking about it.

Jenny does. She's smart, sweet, and kind-hearted, and there's no way she'd ever do anything to hurt Webster, but she can't let go of the thought. Sadly, it doesn't get any better when she's home. As she walks around the house, she inevitably finds herself having to step over Webster from time to time, and she'll struggle with thoughts of driving the heel of her pump into his belly. While many women have at times wanted to do just that to a boyfriend or husband, an innocent dog, one who doesn't ever put the basketball game before you, is another matter entirely. The

People with obsessive bad thoughts (OBT) find themselves focused on things that may be injurious to them, such as jumping from a dangerously high place. (Phanie/ Photo Researchers, Inc.)

vicious cycle of "I know I won't really do these things, but I am thinking about them, so maybe I really will do these things, even though I know I won't really do these things . . ." can be distressing. Counseling and antidepressant meds help Jenny cope, as does her willingness to talk openly about her condition. She's able to laugh about it now, going so far as to call her pumps "dogkillers."

Knocking People Out of Wheelchairs

Grant, a 32-year-old overnight package delivery man, obsesses about knocking people out of wheelchairs. Just for kicks. Obviously, this is a problem when you have to visit a friend in the hospital, a parent in a nursing home, or represent your company at the Jerry Lewis Labor Day Telethon. Grant manages his OBT through counseling and "exposure therapy." This means walking around a hospital, sometimes with his counselor by his side, and confronting his bad thoughts. He's learned that he isn't going to flip an 82-year-old woman who just had a hip replacement out of her wheelchair. At least not without a good reason.

Shouting Out at a Wedding

My pencil-pushing obsession went away, interestingly, just weeks after I had a couple of sessions with a counselor and got my worries out in the open. But then another round of OBT struck. This one was less physically violent but equally upsetting, and a little harder to shake. I suppose that's because it was more "doable"—I could pull it off without injuring someone or ending up in prison. My new OBT? I worried that I might shout something inappropriate during a wedding. This was particularly problematic as I was at the age when *everyone* I knew was getting married, myself included.

Misbehaving at the Reception

I obsessed over my bad thoughts less at the receptions than during the more staid ceremonies, but I still obsessed. That's because, in part, most receptions offer ample opportunities to shout inappropriate things. Take the all-important toasts led by the best man and the maid of honor. The fond retelling of how the couple met and how their best friends will continue to love them even as they embark on a new life triggered my OBT brain. It encouraged me to yell out, "The groom pinched my sister's butt during the Bunny Hop!" or, "The bride doesn't need any sex pointers. She could teach a three-day seminar on the topic!" But I valiantly resisted.

What made it all the more tempting to misbehave at the reception is that such socially twisted behavior is more easily excused when alcohol is flowing freely and relatives who don't typically get along need to make nice with one another. If you're going to fly off the handle, best to have seven gin and tonics to blame it on, right?

Disrupting the Business Meeting

During this same period in my life, I also had to talk my obsessed mind down off the ledge during several business meetings. Nothing will impress a Fortune 500 client and build their confidence quite like dropping your pants and asking to be spanked with a manila file folder, preferably one labeled "Confidential."

I once had an OBT attack while sitting in the audience during a news conference about a new manufacturing facility being built here in Cincinnati. A few carefully chosen words shouted out while the TV cameras were rolling would have allowed me to embarrass myself in front of a crowd equivalent to hundreds of weddings. Thankfully, I held my tongue. And my job.

These urges, too, eventually subsided, and I'm relieved to say I've been OBT-free for more than a decade. I still think bad thoughts now and then, like punching a rude store clerk in the nose, or shouting "I love mayonnaise!" in the middle of a matinee. But that's rare. Still, if we should ever meet, don't hand me a pencil unless you're wearing goggles.

Everyone with OCD Has Both Obsessions and Compulsions

Bradley C. Riemann

Bradley C. Riemann is a doctor and the clinical director of the Obsessive-Compulsive Disorder Center and the Cognitive-Behavioral Therapy Services of Rogers Memorial Hospital in Oconomowoc, Wisconsin. He also supervises a training program for graduate and postgraduate students from around the country in cognitive behavioral therapy in anxiety disorders. The American Psychological Association (APA) defines OCD as a disorder that includes either obsessions or compulsions or both, which allows for a subtype of OCD that includes obsessions only. Riemann and other OCD experts disagree, believing from experience that either compulsions are actually present, although in the form of a thought action and perhaps unnoticed at first by the sufferer, or that true obsession is not present but rather chronic worry or generalized anxiety disorder (GAD).

Obsessive-compulsive disorder (OCD) is diagnostically classified as an anxiety disorder due to its hallmark feature of intense periods of anxiety. The diagnostic criterion for OCD states that an individual

SOURCE: Bradley C. Riemann, "'Pure O'—Fact or Fiction?" OCD Chicago.org, March 29, 2009. Reproduced by permission of the author.

needs to experience either obsessions or compulsions to have OCD (American Psychiatric Association). The inclusion of this "either or" in the definition of OCD allows for the existence of an individual suffering from only obsessions (i.e., "pure obsessional, or "pure O"). This subtype of OCD seems to contradict clinical observations made by many thought leaders in the field of OCD. Meaning that many would say that they have never assessed or treated an individual with pure O, forcing them to conclude that this phenomenon is either quite rare or it simply does not exist. So which is it? The manuals we rely on state that this condition is possible (i.e., fact) yet many leaders in the field say that it doesn't exist (i.e., fiction).

In my own experience, I have had many OCD sufferers who believe (or have been told) that they have pure obsessional OCD. They supposedly only suffer from obsessional thoughts but do nothing in response to them. These individuals will report that they don't do "any of that hand washing or checking stuff and only have the thinking part of OCD" [and] therefore are pure O's.

Obsessions and Compulsions

Obsessions are defined as unwanted thoughts, images, or impulses that generate high levels of anxiety. Common examples of obsessional thoughts are the fear of contamination, doubting, need for exactness or symmetry, harming, or other unacceptable thoughts. Compulsions are some repetitive or ritualistic act that is done to neutralize the obsessional thought, reduce the anxiety that it causes, or is done to somehow prevent a bad event from occurring. These acts can be behavioral (e.g., washing, tapping, physically checking a door lock) or mental (e.g., counting or praying silently in one's head, mentally reviewing an event or conservation). Herein, I believe, lies the root of this controversy.

Although, as stated above, I have met many individuals who initially believed they had pure O subtype OCD

People with obsessional thoughts develop compulsions to neutralize their obsessions. (© BE&W agencja fotograficzna Sp. z o.o./Alamy)

but none of these cases ended up being classified as such. As the definition of compulsions shows us, the "thinking part" of OCD goes well beyond just the obsessional aspect of OCD. Compulsions can be a mental or thinking act as well. They do not have to be something you can see (i.e., a behavior). Counting, praying, repeating words or phrases, or reviewing can all be done in one's head. As a result, they can commonly be mis-defined as obsessions rather than compulsions thus leading one to believe in the pure O subtype of OCD.

A Broader Definition of Compulsions

My stance is that everyone with OCD has both obsessions and compulsions. If we keep the broader definition of compulsions in mind, I have always (without fail) been able to tease out some sort of thought or image that is done in response to the obsession. It may be very brief (e.g., thinking "God is good"), perhaps even outside of the individual's awareness initially, but it is there.

So how can you or your therapist determine which thoughts are obsessions and which are compulsions? It is actually fairly simple. You need to do what we call a "functional analysis" of the thoughts. Don't worry; I am not talking about that kind of "analysis." To perform a functional analysis on your thoughts all you need to do is ask yourself "when I think that thought do I experience an increase in anxiety?" If so, then it is an obsessional thought. Another question to ask yourself is "when I think that other thought does my anxiety go down (or at least was that the goal of the thought)"? If so, then it was a mental compulsion.

Anxiety Producing Thoughts

So what if you (or your therapist) perform this functional analysis and you still conclude that there are anxiety producing thoughts but nothing that follows designed to reduce it? Is this the elusive pure O or perhaps something else? Notice I called these "anxiety producing thoughts" and not obsessions. Typically, when someone presents with thoughts that induce anxiety but do not perform any behavioral or mental compulsions designed to reduce the anxiety, a therapist should consider the possibility of the diagnosis of generalized anxiety disorder (GAD). GAD is a different type of anxiety disorder characterized by excessive and unrealistic worry regarding multiple life areas (American Psychiatric Association). Individuals with GAD have anxiety producing thoughts (e.g., worry), but do not perform any rituals. Common themes of worry in GAD include safety of children, health of family members, financial security, and job performance.

Worry

There is a large difference between obsessions and worry. Obsessions are typically described as "lightning bolts from the blue." An individual who experiences obsessional thoughts will say that one minute they were "minding their own business" and the next minute flooded with unwanted thoughts, images, or impulses that were very

Common Compulsions in OCD

- **Cleaning:** Repeatedly washing one's hands, bathing, or cleaning household items, often for hours at a time

- **Checking:** Checking and rechecking several or hundreds of times a day that the doors are locked, the stove is turned off, the hair dryer is unplugged, etc.

- **Repeating:** Inability to stop repeating a name, phrase, or simple activity (such as going through a doorway over and over)

- **Hoarding:** Difficulty throwing away useless items such as old newspapers or magazines, bottle caps, or rubber bands

- **Repeatedly touching and arranging**

- **Mental rituals:** Endless reviewing of conversations, counting, repetitively calling up "good" thoughts to neutralize "bad" thoughts or obsessions, or excessive praying and using special words or phrases to neutralize obsessions

Taken from: Anxiety Disorders Association of America, *Obsessive-Compulsive Disorder Handbook: A Guide to Breaking Free from OCD, 2008.*

unwanted and unacceptable. Worry, on the other hand, is described as "a rolling thunder." An individual will begin to worry about something and the intensity continues to grow over time. The thoughts are not considered unwanted or unacceptable. In fact, some with GAD would think it would be unacceptable not to worry about these things.

Mislabeled Obsessions

Therefore, in my opinion pure O is fiction. It doesn't exist. In most cases, what we were calling pure O was really the typical mental obsessions with mental compulsions which were being mislabeled as obsessions. In some cases, perhaps the individual who thought they had pure O really didn't even have OCD but had GAD instead. It is also important to keep in mind anxiety disorders commonly co-occur in the same individual. Meaning, that if some of the information regarding GAD was ringing some bells don't automatically jump to the conclusion that you have only GAD and not OCD; people can have both.

> **FAST FACT**
>
> About 5 percent of people have generalized anxiety disorder at some point in their lives, and women are twice as likely to have it as men.

Mental Rituals

From a treatment perspective, individuals with obsessions and mental compulsions are no different than the more typical OCD cases with obsessions and behavioral compulsions. From a clinician standpoint my job is the same and is no more difficult whether the compulsions are behavioral or mental. An exposure hierarchy would be developed and the mental compulsions would be addressed with ritual prevention. However, from a sufferer's standpoint treatment of mental rituals is more difficult. This is because the compulsive thoughts can occur so quickly and seemingly automatically. Our experience is that individuals who are motivated do respond to treatment; however, it may take more time and more intensive therapy.

Hoarding Is a
Form of OCD

Janice Gaston

Hoarding, compulsively saving things, has been in the news since at least 1947 when it contributed to the death of two brothers, one of whom was killed by a pile of junk that fell on him. Here journalist Janice Gaston reports on hoarding for the *Winston-Salem (NC) Journal*. Gaston explains that hoarding is a form of obsessive-compulsive disorder (OCD) and goes beyond being a pack rat. Hoarders fear discarding things. The thought of discarding something makes them extremely anxious, while the act of saving something makes them calm. Dangers of hoarding include an increased risk for fire, injury from falling objects or from tripping on things, unsanitary conditions, and the inability to prepare food. Treatment, if sought, is usually behavior response therapy and antidepressants, but many hoarders do not seek treatment because they do not see that they have a problem or are too embarrassed to ask for help.

SOURCE: Janice Gaston, "Read This, but Do Not Save It!" *Winston-Salem (NC) Journal*, May 6, 2008. © 2008 Media General Communications Holdings, LLC. Reproduced by permission.

If clutter imprisons you, if you feel too embarrassed to let anyone visit your home, if the mess in your house is becoming a health hazard, you probably have a problem. You are most likely a hoarder.

Experts consider hoarding to be a form of obsessive-compulsive disorder, or OCD, an anxiety disorder, said Tommie Jackson, a pastoral psychotherapist in private practice in Winston-Salem. Obsessions are thoughts that people have that bother them, sometimes to an extreme, and compulsions are behaviors that people perform to deal with the anxiety caused by their obsessions. The obsessions are usually random and not related to such real-life issues as work or money stresses, Jackson said. They are inappropriate thoughts that they can't block.

In typical cases of OCD, said Gretchen Brenes, people might be obsessed with whether they turned off their stoves. Brenes is a professor in the department of psychiatry and behavioral medicine at Wake Forest University Baptist Medical Center and a psychologist with a special interest in OCD. "The compulsion is that they repeatedly go to the stove and check it. It's not a problem with their memory. They know good and well that they have turned off the stove." But they feel so much anxiety that perhaps they didn't turn it off properly that they can't handle it and must continue to check.

Hoarders Calm Themselves by Saving Things

"That 20-year-old piece of foam probably will not come in handy," Jackson said, "but you never know. It's an important thing to emphasize that these people do focus on that extremely, extremely small chance that something may happen or that they may need that item or that something bad would happen if they didn't have it."

People might hang on to old newspapers, thinking that they could need the information they contain some day. "You never know when you might want to check

Could I Have a Compulsive Hoarding and Cluttering Problem?

- Do I think I have too much stuff?

- Do friends and family think I have too much stuff?

- Do I have rooms I cannot use because of clutter?

- Do I have to move stuff off the furniture/bed in order to use it?

- Do I often lose things in my clutter?

- Am I reluctant to have people over because of the clutter?

- Do I have trouble getting to my windows, fire escape, and doors?

- Have I fallen over my clutter?

- Do I get anxious when I think someone might take, rearrange, or throw away my things?

- Do I bring things home even though my place is already cluttered?

- Am I afraid I will get in trouble with my landlord because of clutter, or have I already gotten in trouble?

If you have answered "yes" to any of these questions, you may have a problem with compulsive hoarding.

Taken from: Mental Health Association of San Francisco, "Overwhelmed by Too Much Stuff?" 2008.

what the score was for the Appalachian football game in 2007 for homecoming," Brenes said. Knowing that the information is at hand soothes anxiety. "Most don't go back and check that information, but the knowledge that it's there is calming."

Hoarders may save anything from rubber bands to plastic containers, but the most-commonly hoarded items include newspapers, magazines, mail, clothes, books and lists.

Experts with the Obsessive-Compulsive Foundation estimate that 700,000 to 1.4 million hoarders live in the United States.

Recently, actress Delta Burke went public about her problems with depression, OCD and hoarding. In one report, she mentioned that hoarding had run in her family. According to several Web sites devoted to hoarding, researchers have found chromosome anomalies that are linked with hoarding in families with OCD.

Many of us laugh about our tendency to collect clutter and call ourselves pack rats. But pack rats don't let their clutter interfere with their lives. They don't feel secretive or ashamed about the stuff they save. It makes sense to many of us to save napkins with our names printed on them from our weddings. It does not make sense, unless you are a hoarder, to save a napkin from Burger King because you think you might need it some day.

> **FAST FACT**
>
> People with OCD who hoard tend to have more severe OCD symptoms than the general population of OCD sufferers.

Hoarding Comes in Degrees

"If your house is extremely cluttered and there's stuff coming out of all your closets, then you might be a little bit more than a pack rat," Brenes said. "If you are saving items you haven't seen or used in years and have difficulty parting with them, then you're a little bit more than a pack rat." You are most likely on the mild edge of hoarding.

Collectors might save specific items, such as old issues of *Sports Illustrated*. They are proud of their collections and will show them off.

Hoarders might collect every single magazine, catalog and other piece of mail that has ever come into their houses, but they don't talk to others about their piles of paper.

In some instances, according to the Obsessive Compulsive Foundation, hoarders may have severe problems with making decisions and avoiding tasks. The thought of cleaning up and organizing their stuff overwhelms them. They may be perfectionists who are so afraid of washing dishes the "wrong" way that they simply avoid doing it.

Hoarding Is Dangerous

Some people may think of hoarders as simply eccentric. But hoarding can become such a serious problem, Brenes said, that hoarders can face physical danger.

In a famous hoarding case in New York in 1947, two reclusive brothers died in a boarded-up dwelling filled with tons of debris, including tin cans, cardboard boxes and telephone directories. One died of malnutrition. The other smothered when a pile of debris fell on him.

The risk of fire becomes a bigger danger for those who block exits with their junk and fill their homes with flammable items, such as newspapers stacked to the ceilings. One study of elderly hoarders showed that 81 percent of them faced such physical risks as falling, being injured by falling debris, an inability to cook and unsanitary conditions.

Some older people who grew up during the Depression may show a tendency toward hoarding but may not be true hoarders, Brenes said. To go through such deprivation at a young and impressionable age "is certainly something that stays with you through a lifetime," she said.

Hoarding and Treatment

True hoarders rarely seek treatment because they are too embarrassed, according to the OC Foundation. Therapists often hear about hoarding issues from concerned family members.

Hoarding is often treated by cognitive-behavioral therapy, in which a therapist helps the patient change faulty thinking patterns into accurate ones. (Phanie/Photo Researchers, Inc.)

Hoarding is often treated with a type of psychotherapy called cognitive-behavioral therapy, Brenes said. Therapists work to change faulty patterns of thinking into accurate ones. "In layman's terms, if you ask someone how to overcome a fear of water, they will [say] you have to face that fear and eventually get in the water," she said. With hoarding, a therapist might ask patients to do something they fear, such as reading that day's newspaper, then throwing it away.

Some doctors will prescribe antidepressants that are also used to treat anxiety disorders, such as Zoloft, Prozac or Paxil. Such drugs can help decrease the obsessive thoughts that lead people to hoard so that therapy can be more effective, Brenes said.

Hoarding Is Different from OCD

William Hathaway

Reporting for the *Hartford (CT) Courant* newspaper, staff writer William Hathaway explains that while some people have both obsessive-compulsive disorder (OCD) and are hoarders, most hoarders do not have OCD. Hathaway presents a picture of hoarding by interviewing a woman who spent seventy-five thousand dollars on things from the Home Shopping Network, most of which she does not have room to store or is even able to use. The interviewee does not exhibit traits of OCD, except for anxiety about giving or throwing things away. While previously experts thought hoarding was a subtype of OCD, and many practitioners still treat it like OCD, Hathaway reports that new studies show that the brains of hoarders respond differently from the brains of OCD sufferers at the thought of throwing something away. The part of the brain that has to do with decision making is much more active. Hoarders also differ from OCD patients in that talk therapy and antidepressants are less successful treatments for hoarders.

SOURCE: William Hathaway, "The Cluttered Life: People Who Hoard Have Trouble Stopping, but They Might Not Really Be Obsessive-Compulsive, Researchers Believe," *Hartford (CT) Courant*, July 29, 2007. Copyright © 2007 The Hartford Courant. Reproduced by permission.

Yazmine's ranch-style house in the Farmington Valley is more of a giant gift box than a home, a place where she stores holiday ornaments, wooden garden ornamental bridges, art prints from Wal-Mart, dozens of household gadgets, nearly 90 boxes of knickknacks and collectibles, and piles of cloth for draperies and chair covers she never seems to get around to sewing.

Yazmine, like her mother, is a hoarder. She can't throw things away. She can't stop buying things. Keys, bills and product warranties get swallowed by clutter and are never seen again. "My uncle asked, 'Is there any gadget on television that you don't own?'" Yazmine said.

A large, gregarious, middle-aged blonde with an easy laugh, Yazmine says she would like to strike up a romantic relationship, but she fears inviting men over because of embarrassment about her surroundings, the same reason she asked that her real name and hometown be withheld. "Someone not too clingy," she said wistfully of her dream man. "I like my space."

Hoarding Is Different

For decades, most psychiatrists characterized her type of behavior as a symptom of obsessive-compulsive disorder, known as OCD, a malady better known for its tireless hand-washers and incessant counters. But researchers at the Institute of Living in Hartford and elsewhere have concluded that hoarding is fundamentally different from OCD and deserves a place of its own in the pantheon of mental health disorders.

Like eating disorders a quarter-century ago, the problem has gone largely unrecognized, even though it may affect millions of people, said Dr. David Tolin, director of the Anxiety Disorders Center at the Institute of Living and author of *Buried in Treasure*, a book on compulsive hoarding.

Different Brains

Hoarders do not respond to antidepressants and talk therapy, which often work for people with OCD. And imaging studies have shown that when asked to throw away objects, the brains of hoarders and those with OCD respond very differently. "It is a lot more complicated than we thought," Tolin said.

To shed more light on the mystery, Tolin is interviewing hoarders, doing more imaging scans and trying out new treatments. Yazmine saw an advertisement for the study and, on an impulse, applied to be a part of it.

She said that on some days she realizes the objects filling her house might be squeezing out the possibility of a truly fulfilling life. But she doesn't know how to start to become an ex-clutter queen. "I think I can do this," Yazmine said. "But I know I will only get so far before I will need help."

Quitting Is Difficult

The odds are, well, stacked against her. The compulsion to hoard is so strong that some people have rented apartments or even purchased second houses to store their precious stuff.

Many hoarders fixate on an object's potential utility. "They say, 'This will make a great present for Aunt Tilley' or 'This will look good in the flower garden,'" Tolin said. "The object never goes to Tilley or into the garden."

Others tend to personalize objects. Tolin recalls a patient who, on seeing a sofa on the side of the road, said, "It needs me to save it." In the same way, "cat ladies" hoard animals until they're overrun by their pets.

"What is striking is how tenacious this problem is, how very embedded in a person's emotions and behaviors," said Gail Steketee, interim dean of the Boston University School of Social Work, who has studied and treated hoarders. "Their lives are built around these compulsions. It is very hard to dislodge them."

Messy, Not Dirty

Yazmine already had a household full of stuff eight years ago, when she had to decide whether to move her mother's clutter from New Britain into her new home.

A hoarder stands outside his home, where an overflow of his belongings has taken over his front porch. Some hoarders rent additional storage space to store items. (AP Images)

Her mother had Alzheimer's disease and was a life-time hoarder, a fact Yazmine attributes to a childhood of want in post-World War II Europe. Even by Yazmine's none-too-stringent standards, her mother had a lot of "junk"—papers, wrappers, cheap ornaments. And even though her mother's possessions would compete for space with her own things, Yazmine moved truckloads of mom's clutter into her home. She explained that her mother had dropped her wedding ring into one of her boxes. Rather than dig through them, Yazmine decided to take it all.

Hoarding tends to run in families, and some experts suspect it has a genetic component. Yazmine's sister is not a hoarder, but a "neat-nik," married and living in New Jersey. Whenever she comes to visit, Yazmine frantically clears one bedroom, cramming stuff into the already full basement or attic.

Yazmine said her house is messy, but never dirty. The bathroom is clean and so is the kitchen, although papers and possessions that crowd the other rooms tend to overflow onto kitchen counters and desktops in the living room.

Hoarders Do Not Like "Help"

Yazmine accepts criticism for her habit—but she does not easily forgive people who take it upon themselves to mess with her clutter. Even several years after her father's death, Yazmine is still angry about the time he took out her Pfaltzgraff dishware from their box, put them in the kitchen and threw away the box. "That was a wedding present. You need a box to give a present," Yazmine said. "He was de-boxing me. He thought he was helping, but he was really messing up my life."

On most days, she tells herself that life isn't so bad. Her friends who have battled cancer have faced much bigger obstacles than a messy house. She said there are always better things to do with her time than clean up clutter.

But, occasionally, doubts creep in and a subtle sense of shame settles over her. Perhaps, she thinks, she has a problem.

> **FAST FACT**
>
> Research has repeatedly failed to find that hoarders have more characteristics of OCD than nonhoarding OCD patients or other anxiety disorder patients, with the exception of traits of perfectionism and a tendency to get lost in details.

For Everything, a Plan

Yazmine always has a plan for every item crammed into the house, but her plans just never seem to come to fruition. She was going to make a game room in the basement, and has two slot machines and a "Pirates of the

Caribbean" pinball machine already down there. But you can't reach the machines because the floor is covered with material for her sewing and stained-glass projects that haven't been started. A longtime friend, also a hoarder, stores his painting supplies in this room. He has yet to complete an art project.

A few years ago, Yazmine sought help for her problem. Her therapist told her that she had a job and friends and that she seemed well-adjusted. She confided to Yazmine that she, too, likes to collect things. "She asked me if I wanted to go to a tag sale," Yazmine said.

Understanding Hoarders

Hoarders are often charming and gregarious. You couldn't pick one out on a busy street. But open the front door and there is no mistaking them.

In severe cases, hoarders fill up all the living space they can with possessions, making it impossible to gain entrance—or sometimes an exit—from rooms. In one of the more famous hoarding cases, recluse Langley Collyer in the 1930s died in a Harlem brownstone when a tunnel made of tons of newspapers collapsed and crushed him as he attempted to bring food to his disabled brother, Homer, who then starved to death. It took police a week of cleaning to find his body.

Hoarders are also invisible. Their secret is often only uncovered by fire marshals, social workers or probate courts after disaster, complaints of neglect or death.

Compulsive hoarders differ from garden variety pack rats in the same way alcoholics differ from problem drinkers. Hoarders acquire large numbers of possessions that are useless or of limited value and fail to discard them, even when clutter makes it impossible to use living space and leads to constant difficulties in functioning. And they often deny they have a problem.

Like Yazmine, the majority of hoarders show no symptoms of OCD. Only about a quarter of patients with

Hoarding Characteristics in Patients with Compulsive Hoarding Syndrome and Hoarding as a Dimension of OCD

Characteristic	Syndrome	
	Compulsive Hoarding Syndrome	Hoarding as a Dimension of OCD
Type of hoarding		
Common items[a]	Yes	Yes
Bizarre items[b]	No	Yes
Main reason for hoarding	Intrinsic and/or sentimental value	Other obsessional themes
Hoarding related to obsessional themes[c]	No	Yes
Presence of OCD symptom other than hoarding	No	Yes
Age at onset of clutter problem (years)	Early 30s	Mid 20s
Checking behavior associated with hoarding	Rare and mild	Frequent and severe
Obsessions related to hoarding (i.e., catastrophic or magical thinking)	No	Yes
Mental compulsions related to hoarding (e.g., need to memorize and recall discarded items)	No	Yes

[a] Old clothes, magazines, CDs/videotapes, letters, pens, old notes, bills, newspapers, etc.

[b] Feces, urine, nails, hair, used diapers, rotten food, etc.

[c] Fear of catastrophic consequence, need for symmetry/order, need to perform checking ritual because of the fear of losing an important item, etc.

Taken from: Albert Pertuse et al., "Compulsive Hoarding," *American Journal of Psychiatry*, October 2008.

OCD—about 2 million Americans—hoard. But more than three-quarters of hoarders show no signs of OCD. "There are millions of hoarders," Tolin said. "We just don't know how many."

Decisions Are Difficult

Many mental health professionals, if they are familiar with hoarding at all, still treat hoarders as if they have OCD. Recent brain imaging studies suggest a reason hoarders are different.

If you ask a compulsive hoarder and someone with OCD to throw something away, the brains of hoarders show comparatively little activity in an area called the anterior cingulate gyrus, which is involved in decision-making. This suggests that hoarders have problems making a decision about what to do with an object. Stroke patients with damage to the same area of the brain also tend to hoard. The inability to make decisions about a possession tends to spill over into other areas of hoarders' lives as well, Tolin said.

As a group, hoarders tend to be talkative, but in some ways they resemble people with head trauma or attention-deficit disorder, Tolin said. They have trouble concentrating or planning a few steps ahead. And some are like addicts—they seem compelled to acquire possessions.

After the death of her parents a few weeks apart in 2004, Yazmine spent her inheritance, about $75,000, buying items on the Home Shopping Network.

Cannot Throw It Away

When therapists treat people like Yazmine as if they have OCD, most do not respond well, Tolin said. Antidepressants seem to have no effect on their behavior and traditional talk therapy in an office setting has little impact.

In a therapist's office, hoarders will promise to throw things away but seldom do. Instead, therapists must visit the home and convince hoarders that no disasters will befall them if they toss out an item. Experts in hoarding have found that only when they visit a hoarder's home can they sometimes convince patients that they have the ability, piece by painful piece, to actually discard items.

Some, like Yazmine, can be helped by a natural disaster. A few years ago, her garage flooded, swamping her mother's possessions. Helped by her sister, Yazmine managed to throw the debris away. In a box of old Christmas ornaments, they found their mother's wedding ring.

Today, the garage is full again.

Psychedelic Mushrooms May Effectively Treat OCD

Eric Swedlund

An illegal substance may hold hope for the millions of people who suffer from obsessive-compulsive disorder (OCD), reports Eric Swedlund in the *Arizona Daily Star* (Tucson). Results of a small preliminary study by the University of Arizona are positive, with all nine participants finding dramatic relief from their OCD symptoms after ingesting psilocybin, the substance that makes psychedelic mushrooms psychedelic. Although made illegal in 1970, psilocybin and other drugs can be tested under the supervision of the U.S. Drug Enforcement Administration (DEA). Swedlund notes that while millions of people suffer from OCD and currently no medication has produced the same positive results of psilocybin, the study was very small and many questions still need to be answered. Further research may determine whether the substance is safe and effective in the long run.

In a small-scale preliminary study, a UA [University of Arizona] psychiatrist has found that psilocybin, the active agent in psychedelic mushrooms, is effective in relieving the symptoms of people who suffer from severe obsessive compulsive disorder. Dr. Francisco A. Moreno and his colleagues conducted the first FDA-approved clinical study of psilocybin since it was outlawed in 1970. The results are published in the [November 2006] edition of the *Journal of Clinical Psychiatry*. Moreno cautions that the study was simply to test the safety of administering psilocybin to OCD patients. The effectiveness of the drug is still in question until a larger controlled study can be conducted.

FAST FACT

Psychedelics are classified as Schedule 1 drugs by the Drug Enforcement Administration, which outlawed their use outside of a research setting. Exceptions have been made for Native American and Brazilian-based religious groups.

Amazing Relief

Still, in each of the nine patients in the study, psilocybin completely removed OCD symptoms for a period of generally four to 24 hours, with some patients remaining symptom-free for days. "What we saw acutely was a drastic decrease in symptoms," he said. "The obsession would really dissolve or reduce drastically for a period of time." People would report that it had been years since they had felt so good, he said. Provisions and policies for scientific research of controlled substances like psilocybin were included in the 1970 Comprehensive Drug Abuse Prevention and Control Act, which outlawed psilocybin. New research into psilocybin does not reflect any change in government policy, said Rogene Waite, a spokeswoman for the Drug Enforcement Administration. The same review process has governed such research the entire time although researchers may have been hesitant to consider using psilocybin in the past, she said.

More Study Needed

Currently, there is no treatment in the medical literature that eases OCD symptoms remotely as fast, Moreno said. Other drugs take several weeks to show an effect, but the psilocybin was almost immediate. Still, it's not a drug patients could take daily and in any case, doctors don't

know what would happen with repeated use: Would the effects be additive and longer-lasting over time? Or would the effects dissipate as the patient developed a tolerance?

Moreno, who is in "grant-seeking mode," said the next step is to conduct an expanded study. The findings would be far more convincing on the effectiveness of psilocybin in OCD patients, he said. "We're very cautious about making too much of the early results," Moreno said. "I don't want to characterize it as psychedelics are the way to go. Although it seemed to be safe, this was done in the context of supervision by trained professionals in a medical setting. This is not ready to be used by the public just because nine people tolerated it." A spokeswoman for the Food and Drug Administration declined to comment on the research, citing "confidentiality."

Moreno, whose specialty is in treatment resistance, started thinking about the psilocybin study in the mid-1990s after a patient said the only time he was ever free of OCD symptoms was a decade earlier in college when he experimented with psychedelic mushrooms.

Preliminary studies have revealed that using the psilocybin mushroom, a hallucinogen, as a treatment for OCD may have a dramatic effect in relieving OCD symptoms. (**Adam Hart-Davis/Photo Researchers, Inc.**)

The Risks of Psychedelic Mushroom Use

Physical	Psychological
• Nausea	• Hallucinations
• Vomiting	• Inability to discern fantasy from reality
• Muscle weakness	• Panic reactions
• Drowsiness	• Psychosis
• Lack of coordination	

Taken from: National Drug Intelligence Center, U.S. Department of Justice, "Psilocybin Fast Facts."

Similar to Antidepressants

Psilocybin and other drugs in that family work by activating certain serotonin receptors, in some ways similar to the mechanisms of antidepressants used to treat OCD. Moreno examined the medical literature on psilocybin and LSD and found some other cases in which OCD patients reported improvement under similar conditions. He started the study in 2001, gradually recruiting patients through 2004. Under strict rules to guard against complications, Moreno gathered nine OCD patients who had treatment with the typical medications and had prior positive experience with psychedelic drugs. The patients were tested between one and four times, with 29 sessions in all.

They were administered one of four dose levels of psilocybin in the morning and were monitored in a modified office for eight hours. The patients were given eye shades and listened to music, with instructions to turn their attention inward. They were each interviewed at the end of the day about their experiences and kept in the hospital overnight to make sure they had no drug complications. The patients had a range of obsessions and compulsions, including fear of being contaminated, elaborate cleaning rituals, tapping or touching rituals and mental rituals. One patient wouldn't touch the floor with anything but the soles of his shoes. Others would shower for hours or put on pants over and over again until they felt right. "They know it's senseless. They know it doesn't do anything for them, but if they don't do it they become very distraught and very uncomfortable and have a very difficult time functioning," Moreno said. OCD symptoms develop as early as childhood but typically in the teen years. Over time the mental barriers make it hard for patients to lead normal, day-to-day lives.

A Number of People Could Benefit

Leslie Tolbert, UA vice president for research, graduate studies and economic development, said the university's Human Subjects Protection Program sets the rules for all research involving people to ensure the safety of participants and maximize the usefulness of the study. Psilocybin, like any other controlled substance, is heavily monitored. Any further study of psilocybin at the UA would be federally funded and subject to review and oversight at that level as well, she said. "We don't have great treatments out there for OCD and any indication that there is a path to explore for something that would be effective seems an important thing to respond to," Tolbert said. "It's important that if psilocybin, perhaps in lower doses than are hallucinogenic, really has an impact, it's known. It's not a trivial question. There is a huge number of people who could benefit." A few other researchers across the country have been involved in psilocybin research in the last several years, with some looking at the mystical experiences or sense of well-being associated with the drug, others examining its effect on patients with post-traumatic stress disorder and others examining it as a possible treatment for cluster headaches.

Deep Brain Stimulation Effectively Treats OCD

PR Newswire

PR Newswire, a leader in information and news distribution for professional communicators, reports that Medtronic, Inc. has received Conformité Européenne (CE) Mark approval—as well as Food and Drug Administration approval—for a medical device called Reclaim. Reclaim provides deep brain stimulation (DBS) therapy for patients with severe OCD. The device, which is surgically implanted, delivers controlled electrical pulses to certain areas of the brain. DBS Therapy has been used successfully to treat disorders such as Parkinson's disease.

Medtronic today announced that Reclaim® Deep Brain Stimulation (DBS) Therapy has received CE (Conformite Europeene) Mark approval for the treatment of chronic, severe treatment-resistant obsessive-compulsive disorder (OCD). This is the first time that a deep brain stimulation therapy has gained approval in Europe for the treatment of a psychiatric disorder.

SOURCE: PR Newswire, New York: 2009. Copyright © 2009 PR Newswire Association LLC. Reproduced by permission.

Following CE Mark approval, Medtronic will conduct a multi-national post-market study to commence in at least eight sites in Europe. In addition to following any adverse events associated with the therapy, the study will further evaluate improvements seen in OCD symptoms as assessed by the Yale-Brown Obsessive Compulsive Scale (Y-BOCS), before deep brain stimulation to 12 months after.

A New Treatment Hope

Professor Loes Gabriels from the Catholic University of Leuven, Belgium, and lead investigator of the post-market study comments: "For patients with severe OCD who have tried and failed treatment through the treatment algorithm, DBS could result in a significant improvement of a disease that severely impacts on their lives. This study will be important in reinforcing the evidence base of DBS in the treatment of psychiatric conditions."

European centres first pioneered the technique of deep brain stimulation and the Catholic University of Leuven in Belgium was a leading contributor to the clinical evidence which was used to obtain CE mark approval in Europe as well as FDA [Food and Drug Administration] approval in the United States (obtained in February 2009 through a humanitarian device exemption).

Previous research into DBS therapy for OCD, recently published in the journal *Molecular Psychiatry,* revealed clinically meaningful symptom reductions and functional improvement in about two-thirds of patients and demonstrated that a majority of patients moved from a severe OCD rating at the start of the study to a mild or moderate rating at various follow-up points after device implantation.

The studies also highlighted the importance of a multidisciplinary approach to treating OCD with deep brain stimulation therapy.

Prof [Bart] Nuttin, neurosurgeon at the Catholic University of Leuven in Belgium comments: "It is clear that for the best results a multidisciplinary team consisting of a psychiatrist and neurosurgeon plus several other important specialties must be involved when selecting, treating and managing the long-term follow-up for a patient who undergoes deep brain stimulation for OCD."

OCD and DBS

OCD affects 2 percent of the population and it is estimated that for patients with chronic, severe treatment-resistant OCD, more than 1,000 patients per year could benefit from Reclaim DBS Therapy for OCD in Western Europe. Patients with severe OCD, as defined by a Y-BOCS score over 30, and who have tried at least three selective serotonin reuptake inhibitors (SSRIs) without treatment success, may be considered eligible for Reclaim DBS therapy.

The neurostimulators used for Reclaim DBS Therapy are the same as those used to treat common movement disorders like Parkinson's disease and dystonia. However, because the area of the brain targeted for OCD is different, a unique DBS lead has been specially designed by Medtronic.

"Deep brain stimulation therapies were pioneered by Medtronic neuromodulation and to date, with more than 20 years of experience, 60,000 people worldwide have benefited from Medtronic DBS therapy for Parkinson's disease, essential tremor and dystonia," said Karl Schweitzer, vice president for Medtronic's Neuromodulation business in Europe. "This approval marks the world's first steps into DBS for psychiatric disorders and demonstrates how Medtronic continues to lead the way in research, therapy indication expansion, and technology."

Medtronic Reclaim DBS Therapy is indicated for bilateral stimulation of the anterior limb of the internal capsule, AIC, as an adjunct to medications and as an alternative to anterior capsulotomy for treatment of chronic,

> **FAST FACT**
>
> An estimated 25 to 40 percent of all people with OCD do not respond adequately to medication and/or psychological therapies.

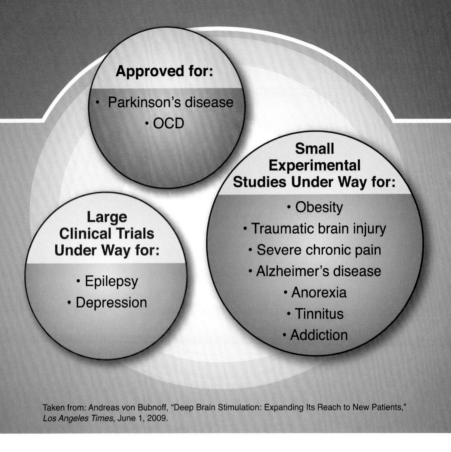

Deep Brain Stimulation: Its Approved and Potential Uses

Approved for:

- Parkinson's disease
- OCD

Small Experimental Studies Under Way for:

- Obesity
- Traumatic brain injury
- Severe chronic pain
- Alzheimer's disease
- Anorexia
- Tinnitus
- Addiction

Large Clinical Trials Under Way for:

- Epilepsy
- Depression

Taken from: Andreas von Bubnoff, "Deep Brain Stimulation: Expanding Its Reach to New Patients," *Los Angeles Times*, June 1, 2009.

severe, treatment-resistant obsessive-compulsive disorder (OCD) in adult patients who have failed at least three selective serotonin reuptake inhibitors (SSRIs).

About Reclaim DBS Therapy

Reclaim DBS Therapy is an adjustable, reversible and non-drug therapy that uses a surgically implanted medical device, similar to a pacemaker, to deliver carefully controlled electrical pulses to precisely targeted areas of the brain. The stimulation can be programmed and adjusted non-invasively (without surgery) by a trained clinician to find the most appropriate type and amount of stimulation for

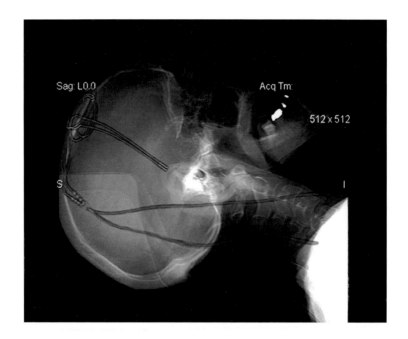

Deep brain stimulation is shown in this X-ray. In this treatment for OCD, two electrodes (blue) are surgically implanted deep in the cerebral hemisphere. **(Medical Body Scans/ Photo Researchers, Inc.)**

each patient to maximize symptom control and minimize side effects.

For OCD and treatment-resistant depression—a further psychiatric disorder which Medtronic is currently exploring with Reclaim DBS therapy in a multi-center randomized clinical trial—the anatomical target in the brain is the anterior limb of the internal capsule (AIC), and more specifically, a region sometimes referred to as the ventral capsule/ventral striatum (VC/VS), which is a central node in the neural circuits believed to regulate mood and anxiety.

About OCD

People with OCD have persistent, upsetting thoughts (obsessions) and use rituals (compulsions) to control the anxiety these thoughts produce. If OCD becomes severe, it can keep a person from working or carrying out normal daily activities. Standard treatments such as medications and cognitive behavioral therapy (CBT) fail to work for a subset of people with OCD.

CHAPTER 3

The Personal Side of OCD

A Teen Boy Battles OCD

Jared Douglas Kant

Jared Douglas Kant is a clinical research assistant at the Massachusetts General Hospital Obsessive-Compulsive Disorder Clinic and Research Unit in Boston. He also suffers from OCD. In *The Thought That Counts,* Kant writes to a teen audience, using a firsthand narrative to describe what it is like to live with OCD. In this excerpt, Kant describes an OCD meltdown. In his middle school locker room, he is overwhelmed and paralyzed by the simple task of changing his clothes for gym class and then grateful for the people who come to his aid.

L ocker rooms are full of disease, or at least they feel that way. So it's no surprise that one of the first times my OCD manifested itself at school involved a locker room. My classmates seemed to like it there. They ran around the room, squirting bottles of cologne

Photo on previous page. OCD sufferers sometimes spend most of their day excessively cleaning their homes. (© **Angela Hampton Picture Library/ Alamy**)

SOURCE: Jared Douglas Kant, *The Thought That Counts: A Firsthand Account of One Teenager's Experience with Obsessive-Compulsive Disorder.* New York: Oxford University Press, 2008. Copyright © 2008 Oxford University Press, Inc. Reproduced by permission of Oxford University Press.

at each other, telling tasteless jokes, and pelting each other with dirty clothes like a cotton snowball fight. But I hated that room. The smell of feet, sweat, and body odor was enough to make me gag.

Some days, the soccer team brought a sizable chunk of the field inside on their cleats, and the dank smell of earth added to the nauseating odors. I would look down and think about how many people had traveled that dirty floor. No matter how much the janitor cleaned, I was still anxious. To protect myself, I usually wore boots, which became my foot armor.

The Combination Lock

At the school I attended for three years beginning in middle school, gym was mandatory for everyone. Each student was assigned a locker with a combination lock. On the first day of gym class, your combination could be found on a piece of paper, like the fortune from a fortune cookie, taped to the lock.

Unfortunately, the combination was composed of three numbers that were arbitrary, not based on any number system in my head. And the knob on the lock had to be turned forward and backward in a pattern that was predetermined, not based on any pattern I felt compelled to follow. If I compulsively turned the knob too far, the tumblers in the lock wouldn't line up, and it wouldn't open. To make matters worse, even when compulsions weren't getting in my way, I had the hardest time figuring out which direction to turn the knob. I later learned that this was related to a math disability. I think everyone in my grade knew my locker combination within a month, because I had to ask for help with the lock so often.

Changing in Public

I wasn't comfortable changing into my gym clothes. The idea of putting on a dirty t-shirt and gym shorts was gross. In addition, the thought of people watching me change clothes made me obsess over what they thought of me. And exposing body parts made me terrified that I would contract some airborne pathogen and fall violently ill. For all these reasons, I waited to change until the others had left the locker room to throw basketballs at each others' heads.

Rules for Dressing

I also had to dress according to very specific rules. If I put on my socks before my shorts, which I was prone to do because I was so repulsed by the dirty floor, then I would have to undress completely and start the process all over again. Needless to say, I was almost always late to gym class.

Locker Room Meltdown

One day, it went too far even by OCD standards—and that's far indeed. I was running later than usual, and everyone else had already scuttled out the double doors leading from the locker room. I began changing into my gym clothes, but somewhere along the line, the anxious thoughts looping through my brain took over, and I lost track of everything else. When I finally snapped out of it, I realized, much to my confusion and distress, that I wasn't wearing any clothes except my socks and shoes. Standing there nearly nude in the middle of the floor, I panicked.

I was terrified that the other students would return to change back into their regular clothes and find me still semi-naked. Yet I had to fight with my brain for several minutes to put on even a marginally decent number of clothes. Finally, I collapsed onto the floor, crying. Unable to shake my mind free from obsessions, I felt mentally stuck and physically rooted to the ground. Unless someone I trusted could assure me that it was perfectly fine to keep dressing, I wasn't going to budge from that spot. I needed reassurance from a person of authority that a cataclysm wasn't going to happen or, if it did, that it would have little or nothing to do with the way I got dressed.

For OCD sufferers like the author, a school locker room can be a terrifying place. (© Emilio Rodriguez/ QuickImage Productions S.L./Alamy)

A Cry for Help

Eventually, I started yelling to see if anyone—by that point, it didn't matter who—would hear me and come to bail me out from my personal jail. My voice became hoarse from yelling so much, I sobbed onto the dirty floor, and I wondered if I was doomed to stay on that nasty spot until I starved to death or caught some fatal illness from the filth.

At that moment, the coach happened to go into his office, and he heard me cry out. He came into the locker room, concerned and confused. Although he didn't know much about OCD, the coach, like all the faculty, was aware that I had something wrong with my head, that I would get scared for no apparent reason, and that I would often need the help of adults, whether I liked it or not.

Looking back, I think the coach must have been considering the rules about contact with a student, as it was rather obvious that what I really needed was a hug. In the end, I think he weighed the risk and decided to hell with it. He came over, knelt beside me, and wiped my tears until I looked up in choking sobs. Then he asked me what had happened. To be honest, I didn't really know, and I told him as much.

Just Following Orders

I wonder in retrospect how that must have sounded. I was crying on a grimy locker room floor, disoriented and anxious. Unaware of how I had reached the point of immobility, I was still clinging to the orders in my head that said to stay put until someone else told me what to do.

I cried for a long time. Another student—a good-hearted friend who cared about my condition and wanted to help—wandered into the locker room. Ironically, I think he was hoping to skip out of extra laps around the gym for some insubordination. Luckily for him, good Samaritans are more in demand than discipline cases. The coach told my friend to contact the other gym teachers and explain that the boys' locker room was temporarily closed and gym students would be excused from other classes until they could change.

A Community of Support

The coach sat with me and coached me through getting dressed. He assured me that no harm would befall me or anyone else if I opened my locker and finished putting

> **FAST FACT**
>
> Studies show that one-half to two-thirds of adult OCD cases start in childhood.

on my clothes. When I was finally dressed, I felt a ripple of fatigue wash through my body. It's incredibly draining to put that much effort into anything. I collapsed against the coach and cried. He asked what else he could do to help, and I thanked God for this man who had wandered through by sheer providence and helped me overcome the immobilizing effects of anxiety.

At last, I was ready to leave. Unseen by the other students, I exited the locker room and went to my advisor's office, where I could catch my breath and get my bearings. After I was gone, the locker room was reopened. My classmates changed into their regular clothes without ever realizing how close they had come to witnessing one of my less-than-stellar moments. That was the scariest part of the whole disease for me. OCD was unpredictable, awkward, and embarrassing. It would crop up in the most inconvenient places—although I think it's safe to say there's really no such thing as a good place for an OCD attack.

A Teen Girl Struggles with Scrupulosity

Jennifer Traig

Jennifer Traig is perhaps best known for her memoirs, *Devil in the Details: Scenes from an Obsessive Girlhood* and *Well Enough Alone: A Cultural History of My Hypochondria*. This viewpoint is an excerpt from her first memoir, *Devil in the Details*. In the book she recounts her life with scrupulosity, a form of obsessive-compulsive disorder (OCD) that centers on religious observance. This excerpt is from the first few pages of the book, which introduce the reader to the concept of scrupulosity through vivid descriptions of Traig's own bizarre religious compulsions.

My father and I were in the laundry room and we were having a crisis. It was the strangest thing, but I couldn't stop crying. And there were a few other weird things: I was wearing a yarmulke [Jewish skullcap] and a nightgown, for one, and then there were my hands, red and raw and wrapped in plastic baggies. My lip was split. There were paper towels under my feet. And weirdest of all, everything I owned seemed to be in the washing machine, whites and colors, clothes and shoes, barrettes and backpacks, all jumbled together. Huh.

"Huh," my father said, examining the Reebok Esprit Hello Kitty stew churning through permanent press. "You want to tell me what happened here?"

Wasn't it obvious? The fumes from the bacon my sister had microwaved for dessert had tainted everything I owned, so now it all had to be washed. But this sort of rational explanation hadn't been going over well with my father lately. I scrambled to think of another, turning lies over in my mouth: it was homework, an experiment; it was performance art, a high-concept piece protesting the consumerization of tweens. I glanced up at my father and down at the machine, then dragged my baggied wrist under my nose and exhaled. "I don't know."

Scrupulosity

We didn't know. Many years later we would learn that what happened was a strange condition called scrupulosity, a hyper religious form of obsessive-compulsive disorder. It hit me when I was twelve and plagued me, off and on, throughout my teens, making every day a surprising and mortifying adventure. The disease manifested itself in different ways, but they were always, always embarrassing. Sometimes I had to drop to my knees and pray in the middle of student council meetings, and sometimes I had to hide under the bleachers and chant psalms. Sometimes I couldn't touch anything and sometimes I had to pat something repeatedly. Sometimes I had to wash my hands and sometimes I had to wash someone else's. Sometimes I had to purify my binders. Sometimes I had to put all my things in the washing machine.

Scrupulosity is also known as scruples, a name I much prefer. Scruples sounds like it could be a pesky, harmless condition: "I ate some bad clams last night, and today I've got the scruples." Scruples is cute and saucy. "Oh, you and your scruples," I imagined my date saying, laughing at the coy way I examined my lunch for spiritual contaminants. Scruples also evokes the fabulous Judith Krantz novel that would lead me to expect a far different disorder, one in which my mental illness compelled me to fulfill the fantasies of Beverly Hills debauchees—for a price.

A Small Sharp Stone

But it's none of that. In fact, *scruple* is the Latin word for a small sharp stone. Originally this denoted a measure; the idea was that the sufferer was constantly weighing the scales of her conscience. I imagine a pebble in a shoe, perhaps because I was hobbled by constant nagging worries and by the undersized pointed flats I wore to punish myself. They pinched and chafed and matched nothing I owned, but weren't nearly as uncomfortable as the doubts that plagued me every second of every day.

Scrupulosity is sometimes called the doubting disease, because it forces you to question everything. Anything you do or say or wear or hear or eat or think, you examine in excruciatingly minute detail. Will I go to hell if I watch HBO? Is it sacrilegious to shop wholesale? What is the biblical position on organic produce? One question leads directly to the next, like beads on a rosary, each doubt a pearl to rub and worry. Foundation garments, beverages, reading material: for the scrupulous, no matter is too mundane for a dissertation-length theological interrogation. Oh, we have fun.

Growing Compulsions

But it was 1982, and we didn't know any of this then. We didn't know what this was or where it had come from. It had come out of nowhere. Well, there were things. There was the fact that I'd been having obsessive-compulsive impulses since preschool. These had been stray and occasional, and while my parents may have thought it was strange that I couldn't stop rearranging the coasters, they didn't think it was anything worth treating. The compulsions had grown with me, however, and now they loomed like hulking, moody preteens. There was also the fact that I'd been systematically starving myself for a year and was no longer capable of making any kind of rational decision. I sometimes wore knickers and pumps, wore fedoras and a vinyl bomber jacket to *seventh grade* setting myself up for the kind of ridicule that takes years of therapy and precisely calibrated medications to undo. No, I was in no condition to make rational decisions, no condition at all.

> **FAST FACT**
>
> Scrupulosity is present in some form in about one of every ten cases of OCD.

Religious Compulsion

And into this mire had come halachah, Jewish law. I had begun studying for my bat mitzvah, twelve years old and a little bit scattered and crazy, and suddenly here were all these wonderful rules. They were fantastic, prescribing one's every movement, giving structure to the erratic compulsions that had begun to beat a baffling but irresistible tattoo on my nervous system. Halachah and latent OCD make a wonderful cocktail, and I was intoxicated. Suddenly I wasn't just washing; I was purifying myself of sin. I wasn't just patting things; I was laying on hands. Now my rituals were exactly that: rituals.

And my gosh, it was fun. The endless chanting, the incessant immersing of vessels—I couldn't get enough. The obsessive behavior quickly evolved from a casual hobby to an all-consuming addiction, a full-time occupation. It happened so fast. One day I was riding bikes to McDonald's like a normal kid; the next, I was painting the lintels [door posts] with marinade to ward off the Angel of Death.

Food Compulsions

I don't remember what came first, but I think it was the food. At this point I'd been having problems with food in an obsessive but secular way for about a year. I had begun eliminating foods from my diet, first sugar and shortening, and then cooked foods, then food that had been touched by human hands, then processed foods, and then unprocessed. By January we were down to little more than dried fruit, and my nails were the texture of string cheese.

But then came these lovely laws to give shape to my dietary idiosyncrasies. It was so sudden and unexpected, this revulsion to pork and shellfish, to meat with dairy. I hadn't asked for it, but here it was. Suddenly I was keeping kosher. I was sort of keeping kosher. I was afraid to tell my parents, so I was hiding it, spitting ham into napkins, carefully dissecting cheese from burger, pepperoni from pizza.

"Is there a reason you're hiding that pork chop under your plate?" my mother wanted to know.

Jennifer's religious scrupulosity made her suddenly revulsed by non-kosher foods such as shellfish. (© age fotostock/SuperStock)

"Oh, I'm just tenderizing it," I lied, thwacking it with the Fiestaware.

"Is there something wrong with the shrimp?" my father inquired.

"Seafood recall, they said on the news. You all can play food poisoning roulette if you like, but I'm giving mine to the cat."

The food could have kept me busy forever, but I was ambitious. One by one, things fell away. I would wake up and know: today, no television, it's blasphemous. Then: no more reading *Seventeen,* it's immodest, it's forbidden. A partial list of things I considered off-limits: exfoliation, hair color, mix tapes, lip gloss. Oh, I had so much energy, and there were so many laws I could take on, and when I ran out I would just make up my own.

The fact that I had no idea what I was doing held me back not at all. Despite six years of Hebrew school and a bat mitzvah crash course, I knew next to nothing about daily Jewish practice. I'd retained a couple folk songs and some Hebrew swear words, but that was about it. The only source texts I had were a King James Bible, an encyclopedia, and the collected works of [Jewish authors] Chaim Potok and Herman Wouk in paperback.

But this was enough. The Bible alone was chock-full of minute instructions, obscure decrees banning the plucking of this and the poking of that. It was these small, specific directives I favored. I was less interested in big guidelines like commandments than in the marginalia of Jewish practice, the fine print, the novelty laws and weird statutes. Had my impulses been secular, I would have observed the funny forgotten ordinances on the law books banning the chewing of gum by false-mustache wearers or the dressing up of one's mule.

As it was I zeroed in on the biblical laws governing agriculture and livestock. Later, as I grew older and more disturbed, I would focus on the laws concerning contamination by death and bodily fluids, but for now it was plants and pets. We did not have any crops, but we had a lawn, and that was close enough. I contrived to leave the corners unmown so the poor could come and glean. I imagined hordes of kerchiefed, unwashed peasants descending to gather sheaves of crabgrass at dawn. "Oh, thank you, Jennifer the Righteous!" they would cry, their dirty faces shining with happiness, blades of grass caught in their blackened teeth.

They never showed up, but I was undeterred. The Bible said, and I did.

A Teen Overcomes OCD with Exposure and Response Prevention Therapy

Fred Penzel

Fred Penzel, executive director of Western Suffolk Psychiatric Services in Long Island, New York, is a licensed psychologist who has specialized in obsessive-compulsive disorder (OCD) since 1982. He is the author of *Obsessive-Compulsive Disorders: A Complete Guide to Getting Well and Staying Well*. Here he writes about one of his former patients, a teen with OCD characterized by obsessive sexual identity thoughts. Secretly fearing that he is gay, the previously outgoing teen throws away his bodybuilding books, stops hanging out with friends, and loses interest in school. Penzel, an experienced therapist, guesses what the teen is going through and gets him to talk. With exposure and response prevention therapy (ERP), the teen conquers his doubts and regains his self-confidence.

When I first saw Michael, I couldn't help but notice just how depressed he looked. The red-haired strongly-built seventeen-year-old could hardly hold his head up. His parents said that he

SOURCE: Fred Penzel, "The Boy Who Didn't Know Who He Was," Western Suffolk Psychiatric Services. WestSuffolkPsych.homestead .com/TeenThoughts.html. Reproduced by permission.

had been really down for several weeks, but no one knew why, and he wasn't helping either. He couldn't seem to come up with the energy to get to school, and preferred to stay in his room, alone. He had been a good student, enjoyed playing on his school's lacrosse team, and was heavily involved in student government. At a time when he should have been thinking about choosing colleges to apply to, he seemed to have dropped out of life. Some possible clues were his parents' report that he had suddenly thrown away his prized collection of bodybuilding magazines, and the fact that he seemed to be avoiding all contact with his guy friends. Another clue was that his father suffered from OCD [obsessive-compulsive disorder] which was particularly interesting to me, as the disorder sometimes appears to run in some families. Finding out what was going on here would be my first, and probably most difficult task, since he was the only one who could help solve this mystery.

Michael and I sat across from each other, with him slumped forward in his chair, his head down, and his hands clasped together. I tried to engage him in some small talk to break the ice. All I got in return were some one-syllable answers. "Is there anything you want to tell me?" I asked. "Nope," was the reply. His whole manner seemed to say that he was also really anxious. Maybe it was the way he chewed his lips and drummed his foot.

A Therapist's Intuition

As we therapists sometimes do, I decided to take a chance and act on intuition—just take a shot in the dark based on what evidence I had. I knew it was risky, because if I was wrong, he might refuse to talk with me any further. I thought I had it right, though, based on the clues I had. "Michael," I said suddenly, "Are you

> **FAST FACT**
>
> A September 2007 article in *Comprehensive Psychiatry* indicates that OCD victims with obsessive sexual, religious, and aggressive thoughts experience them significantly earlier than OCD victims with other kinds of thoughts.

worried that you might be gay?" With that, he jumped back in his chair, his eyes wide. It was as if someone had given him a jolt of electricity. "What? How did you know that?" he gasped. "Nobody knows that. Nobody!" I went further. "Is that why you threw out your magazines?" I asked. He nodded at me. I had seen many cases like this over the past twenty-odd years, so I decided to pull out all the stops and really get things moving, now that I had his attention.

"Let me guess," I said, leaning forward. "One day you were doing something you always do, and suddenly you started to pay attention to yourself in a different way. As you focused on yourself, the thought suddenly came into your head, "Maybe this means I'm gay. How do I really know I'm not?" I kept on, "Since then, you keep checking yourself, you know, like looking at guys or girls and trying to see who you're attracted to. Maybe you watch the way you talk, or walk, or move your hands, to see if you do these things the way a gay or straight person would. How am I doing so far, Mike?" He stared at me and answered, "I feel creeped out, like you're reading my mind."

A Different Kind of OCD

I went on to explain that I definitely didn't have ESP (as far as I knew), but that he was suffering from a very common form of obsessive-compulsive disorder, one that doesn't get talked about very much, and certainly not a lot by people his age. Many people with obsessive sexual identity thoughts shared the particular symptoms I had outlined, so they weren't very hard to guess at. I related to him that at one time, a few years ago, I actually found myself treating six different people at once for this type of OCD, and that we had even held a support group meeting just for this group. I added that these thoughts weren't confined to heterosexual people, and that I had even treated a gay patient who was troubled by obsessive thoughts that he might be straight.

Sudden Doubt

Michael went on to confirm that his doubtful thoughts of being gay came on suddenly one day when he was looking through one of his bodybuilding magazines. He remembered looking at one picture in particular and thinking, "I wonder if I find this guy attractive?" With that, he suddenly became very anxious and horrified that he could have such a thought. He also found that in the days following, he couldn't get the thought out of his head.

What made things worse, was that the other guys in school had a habit of teasing each other about being gay, a not unusual occurrence. Remarks that he used to shrug off now became very frightening. "What if they really can tell?" he remembered asking himself. He found himself avoiding his usual crowd. He threw away the bodybuilding magazines. He stopped going to school. Nothing helped. It seemed like the harder he worked to avoid thinking about whether or not he was gay, the more he would think about it. "But I'm not gay," he emphasized, "I'm not attracted to guys, so why am I thinking this? I've never been attracted to guys!" He paused for a moment. "But the thoughts seem so real."

A Matter of Brain Chemistry

I explained to Michael that these obsessive questions were not "real" questions, and the thoughts were not "real" thoughts. These things that seemed so real were the result of problems with his brain chemistry, and that there were no real answers to his doubts, so no matter how hard he checked himself and his behaviors and thoughts, he would not be able to erase the doubt. The OCD (once known as "The Doubting Disease") would not let him. I told him that the thoughts were, after all, just thoughts, no matter how creepy they were, and that they really had no power to make him anxious.

The truth was that he was actually making himself anxious. The proof of this was that even people who recovered from OCD would still report unpleasant thoughts, but also add that the thoughts no longer made them anxious. Why? Because with the help of therapy, they had faced the thoughts and built up a tolerance for them, to the point where they no longer produced a reaction. "The real problem is not the thoughts," I said, "The problem is what your attempts to control your anxiety are doing to your life and your ability to live it."

Facing the Doubts

Another thing I tried to emphasize to him was that it was not unusual for people to sometimes get doubtful thoughts about their sexuality, but that people without OCD were better able to decide how they really felt about these things, and could eventually put the thoughts aside. "Our goal," I told him, "will be to learn to gradually face the thoughts and resist doing compulsions long enough for you to learn the truth about all this. You will have to face a lot of doubt and feel as if you are taking risks at times, but if you stick with it, you will gradually become desensitized to the thoughts, and they will no longer seem to have any power over you." This was clearly a lot to think about, and Michael would need the next few sessions to really digest all this.

One of the really maddening qualities of OCD is that it can make a person doubt the most basic things about themselves, things no one would ever normally doubt. Even their sexual identity could be questioned. Sufferers will go to great lengths to overcome this doubt even ruining their lives through their desperate actions. Doing compulsions, such as repeated questioning, avoiding things, looking for reassurance, and checking, can be rewarding in the short run, and this is what keeps the problem going. By staying away from the things that make them anxious, sufferers only keep themselves sensitive to these things. Also, this only helps for a little while, and before long, the doubt returns, as it always does. Fortunately, this process also works in reverse, or as a favorite saying of mine goes, "If you want to think about it less, think about it more."

Michael had been attempting to control his anxiety chiefly by avoiding—throwing out his magazines, avoiding his friends, and not going to school. He also kept double-checking his own thoughts to see if he really believed them. He eventually revealed that he also would alternately look at other boys and then at girls, trying to decide whom he was more attracted to. He, himself, admitted that even when these things did work (and often they only raised more questions) the relief only lasted a short time.

Staring Down Anxiety

After learning much more about Michael and his life, we began to prepare to do the behavioral therapy that would be the main part of our treatment. The specific type of therapy we would be doing is known as "Exposure and Response Prevention." In this type of behavioral therapy, the person voluntarily and gradually exposes themselves to greater levels of the things that bother them, and at the same time, agrees to resist doing the compulsive activities that they have been using to make themselves less anxious. The purpose of all this is for them to learn that if they just stay with what makes them anxious long enough, they will come to see the truth of things that these are only meaningless thoughts, and that the anxiety will gradually diminish even if they do nothing. The ultimate goal is for a person to be able to tell him- or herself, "Okay, so I can think about these things, but I don't have to do anything about them."

Identifying Obsessions and Compulsions

As a first step in treatment, we identified all of Michael's various obsessive thoughts concerning being gay, and then all the different compulsions he was using to try to

A number of support groups offer programs in exposure and response prevention therapy for obsessive-compulsive eaters. (AP Images)

control the anxiety that resulted from the thoughts. Next, we listed all the situations we could think of that would make him anxious. These included such things as being around his friends, having his friends joke about being gay, hugging another guy friend, going to a movie with just another guy, looking at pictures of attractive guys or girls, watching romantic scenes in movies, just hearing the word "gay" or similar words, seeing gay characters on TV or in movies, looking at gay magazines, visiting gay websites, etc. We then tried to assign number values, from 0 to 100 to each of these situations, to help us to see what was worse than what.

Starting Small

I told Michael that together, we would create a program especially for him, using the items on this list. We would start with challenging situations that he rated at about a 20, and work upward from there. I helped him pick several lower level items, and also recorded an audiotape for him to listen to several times per day. I explained that this was an Exposure Tape, designed to raise his anxiety to a moderate level, and to get him to "Think about it more." He laughed a bit when I told him, "You can't be bored and scared at the same time." The tape was a two-minute recording of me, talking in a general way about how some people couldn't be sure of their sexual preferences, and turning out to be different than they thought they were. He found this definitely caused some anxiety, but he believed he would be able to listen to it. He would keep listening to it until it became boring. Later tapes would actually tell him that he possibly was gay, and even later ones would tell him he definitely was. I planned for him to eventually record his own tapes, in which he would agree that he was gay, and would soon "come out" and go public. I also stressed that it would become increasingly important for him to agree with his thoughts. This would probably be the single most important assignment we would do, and that we would be doing it all through the therapy. As I sent him on his way with his first list of assignments, I told him that he would see that it wouldn't be as bad as he feared. I added that the worst day of the therapy was the day before you start.

Making Progress

Michael seemed truly surprised at the end of the first week when he came in and told me that the tape really had become boring, and that he was ready for a new one. He seemed somewhat less anxious overall, and proud that he had made it through the first round of homework. Week by week, he worked his way through the list. He gradually became more able to say things he feared to say, to look at pictures he disliked looking at, to listen to words he feared to hear, and to imagine things he really didn't want to imagine. Some things were a struggle for him to stay with, as they represented his worst doubts. To his credit, he stuck with them, and refused to give up, even when he didn't get instant results. He was developing trust in what he was doing. I could tell that he was improving when he was finally able to joke about his thoughts. At one session, he came wearing a pink shirt. "Do you know why I'm wearing this?" he said, raising his eyebrows. "Why?" I asked him. "Because I'm gay," he answered, with a grin. "Didn't you know?" I knew we were winning.

The day finally came when we had arrived at the end of Michael's list. He was no longer avoiding anything, and the worst things on his list no longer seemed to have any effect on him. He could tolerate all of them, and didn't feel the need to run away or avoid them. I showed the list to him to remind him of where he had started out. As he looked it over, he said, partly to himself, "I can't believe these things made me nervous." He added, "I really didn't enjoy doing some of the things you had me do, but I'm glad I did them. I don't have all that nasty stuff filling up my head."

A Continual Process

I told him that the job was only half done. "What do you mean?" he asked, looking puzzled. "Now you have to stay this way," I answered. "Consider yourself officially in recovery," I announced. "But your work isn't over. This means that you will have to do maintenance from this point on. When thoughts on the topic of being gay come up (and they will), you will have to continue to agree with them, and not go back to doing any of the things you used to do before, the ones that only made things worse. People who go back to those kinds of solutions wind up with a relapse. Like the therapy, doing maintenance will get easier as time goes on. It will become second nature."

I tried to leave him with the idea that this next phase would be just as important as the first one was. I stressed that OCD was a chronic problem, which means that even though you can recover, you are not "cured." In a way, it's kind of like having asthma or diabetes. "The people who relapse," I told him, "are the ones who think they are cured." "Don't worry," Michael replied, "I worked too hard to just give it up like that." He was as good as his word. He went off to college not long after, and several e-mails he sent me indicated that he had learned his behavioral therapy well. Even the pressures of school couldn't get him to go back. As of his last message, things were fine.

GLOSSARY

autoimmune response	Reaction in which the immune system mistakes body cells for invaders and attacks them.
basal ganglia	Brain area that triggers and controls voluntary movement.
behavioral therapy	A way of treating psychological problems by teaching patients how to change their present behavior.
body dysmorphic disorder (BDD)	Strong, persistent preoccupation with an imagined or slight physical defect.
caudate nucleus	Component of the basal ganglia; helps regulate thoughts and voluntary movement by separating important information from unimportant information.
cognitive-behavioral therapy	A way of treating psychological problems by identifying irrational thoughts and replacing them with rational ones.
compulsions	Rituals that a sufferer performs to counteract obsessions.
deep brain stimulation	A type of neurosurgery in which electrodes are implanted in the brain.
exposure and response prevention (ERP)	A type of behavioral therapy in which the patient is exposed for a prolonged time to a fear-triggering situation but is prevented from performing compulsive rituals.
hierarchy	A list of situations that cause a sufferer anxiety, arranged in order from least to most anxiety-provoking.
hypochondriasis	Preoccupation with the fear of having a serious illness, based on misinterpretation of bodily symptoms.
neuron	A nerve cell.

neurosurgery	Surgery involving the brain or nervous system.
neurotransmitter	Chemical messenger that delivers signals from one neuron to the next.
obsessions	Disturbing and unwanted thoughts, images, or impulses that arise repeatedly.
obsessive-compulsive disorder (OCD)	An anxiety disorder involving obsessions and compulsions.
obsessive-compulsive spectrum disorders (OCSDs)	Disorders suspected of being related to OCD.
orbito-frontal cortex	Part of the brain's frontal lobes; organizes and interprets information.
PANDAS (pediatric autoimmune neuropsychiatric disorders associated with streptococcal infections)	Condition in which children develop OCD symptoms following a strep throat infection.
positron emission tomography (PET)	A type of imaging study that detects radiation from inside the body and translates it into a computerized image.
psychiatrist	A medical doctor trained to treat mental disorders with medication.
psychoanalysis	A treatment method based on the belief that current psychological problems are caused by earlier experiences.
psychologist	A mental health professional who treats psychological disorders by helping patients change their behavior or way of thinking.
psychotic disorder	A mental disorder in which the sufferer loses contact with reality.
schizophrenia	A psychotic disorder characterized by loss of contact with reality and disorganized speech or behavior.

serotonin	A type of neurotransmitter believed to be involved with OCD.
serotonin-reuptake inhibitors (SRIs)	Medications that affect serotonin activity in the brain.
thalamus	Brain area that receives and transmits messages from one brain area to another.
therapist	A person who is trained and licensed in a particular type of treatment.
tic	A sudden, repeated movement or vocalization that sufferers feel an irresistible urge to perform.
Tourette's syndrome	A neurological disorder that involves both motor and vocal tics.
transcranial magnetic stimulation	A procedure in which magnetic pulses are sent through the skull to affect brain activity.
trichotillomania	Compulsive hair pulling.
Yale-Brown Obsessive Compulsive Scale (Y-BOCS)	A scale that measures the severity of OCD symptoms.

CHRONOLOGY

First Century   Plutarch describes obsessive superstitions about Greek gods Apollo, Hera, and Aphrodite, which may be an early report of scrupulosity.

Sixth Century   John Climacus describes obsessional blasphemous thoughts that occur while praying, attributing them to demons.

Early Middle Ages   Demonic or satanic possession is believed to be the cause of many obsessions, especially blasphemous and sexual obsessions, and exorcism by priests is seen as the cure.

1400s   The term "scrupulosity" begins to appear in Catholic theological writing, particularly in the writings of three scholars: John Gerson, chancellor of the University of Paris; John Nider, dean of the University of Vienna; and Archbishop Antoninus of Florence.

Early 1500s   Christian reformer Martin Luther suffers from scrupulosity, fearing that his confessions of sin are never adequate.

Early 1600s   Shakespeare's *Macbeth* depicts Lady Macbeth obsessively washing her hands. The depiction reflects the religious worldview of the day, connecting obsession to guilt.

1660 Jeremy Taylor, bishop of Down and Connor, Ireland, referring to obsessional doubts, writes about scruples: "[A scruple] is trouble where the trouble is over, a doubt when doubts are resolved."

1666 John Bunyan, in his book *Grace Abounding*, describes his spiritual struggles and blasphemous thoughts in terms that would be recognized today as scrupulosity.

1700s Medical explanations for obsessions and compulsions are more acceptable, but treatment is limited to blood-letting, laxatives, and enemas.

Samuel Johnson, author of the *Dictionary of the English Language*, exhibits compulsive behaviors such as tapping and walking rituals, according to his biographer James Boswell.

1700s–1800s Physicians describe a greater variety of obsessions and compulsions, including washing, checking, fear of germs, fear of syphilis, and one mother's obsessional thoughts of harming her child.

Asylums appear, and many mentally ill, including those with obsessions and compulsions, are institutionalized.

1838 French psychiatrist Jean-Étienne Esquirol publishes *Des Maladies Mentales*, in which he describes obsessions as a form of partial insanity.

1857 Benedict Morel challenges the conventional understanding of obsessions and compulsions, stating that no accounting is being made for the anxiety that accompanies the compulsive behaviors.

1861	French neurologist Paul Broca discovers that brain function, particularly speech function, is localized.
1862	Henri Dagonet, continuing the French psychoanalytic tradition, categorizes obsessive-compulsive symptoms as impulsive insanity.
1894–1895	The journal *Brain* arranges a forum among five experts to discuss obsessions and compulsions.
Late 1800s	Obsessions and compulsions are classified as neuroses rather than psychoses. Sufferers are less frequently institutionalized in asylums.
	Some physicians begin treating obsessions and compulsions with medications, including bromide, opium, morphine, and low doses of arsenic.
Early 1900s	Freud uses the term *Zwangsneurose*. Translated in the United States as "compulsion" and in England as "obsession," the term "obsessive-compulsive disorder" (OCD) is adopted as a compromise.
1909	Sigmund Freud publishes his case study of "the Rat Man," theorizing that the man's obsessive neurosis stemmed from childhood psychosexual issues and could be cured by psychoanalysis. Treatment begins to focus on unconscious conflicts at the root of behaviors rather than the behaviors themselves.
1949	Portuguese neurologist Egas Moniz, who applies Broca's theory of localization to madness, wins a Nobel Prize for inventing the lobotomy.

1949   Neurologist Robert Heath begins to explore deep brain stimulation (DBS) and continues his research over several decades.

1950s   New medications to treat brain disorders such as schizophrenia and depression lead to a decline in the number of lobotomies performed.

1953   B.F. Skinner pioneers behavioral therapy, which will eventually overcome psychoanalysis as the leading treatment for OCD.

Late 1950s   More than thirty thousand Americans have been lobotomized for various maladies, including, but not limited to, homosexuality, mental retardation, and criminal insanity.

1960s–1970s   Learning theories do not fully explain obsessive behavior but do lead to some helpful treatments for obsessive rituals.

1967   The drug clomipramine (Anafranil) is reported to be effective for treating OCD. By the 1980s more than fifteen scientific studies affirm its effectiveness.

Late 1960s–Mid-1970s   The federal Law Enforcement Assistance Administration provides grants to researchers studying brain implants as well as other methods of behavioral modification.

Mid-1970s   Senate hearings shed light on questionably ethical uses of psycho-surgical techniques, including brain stimulation, which then falls out of favor.

1980s   Medical causes are the most accepted explanation for OCD. Cognitive-behavioral therapy, medication, and psychosurgical procedures such as deep brain stimulation are employed in a more successful treatment of OCD.

1987   French neurosurgeon Alim-Louis Benabid discovers that electrical stimulation to the thalamus stops the shaking caused by Parkinson's disease.

2002   Medtronic Inc. receives FDA approval for a brain stimulation device for Parkinson's disease.

2009   Medtronic Inc. receives FDA approval for a brain stimulation device for OCD.

ORGANIZATIONS TO CONTACT

The editors have compiled the following list of organizations concerned with the issues debated in this book. The descriptions are derived from materials provided by the organizations. All have publications or information available for interested readers. The list was compiled on the date of publication of the present volume; the information provided here may change. Be aware that many organizations take several weeks or longer to respond to inquiries, so allow as much time as possible.

American Psychiatric Association (APA)
1000 Wilson Blvd.
Ste. 1825
Arlington, VA 22209-3901
(703) 907-7300
Web site: www.psych.org

An organization of psychiatrists dedicated to studying the nature, treatment, and prevention of mental disorders, the APA helps create mental health policies, distributes information about psychiatry, and promotes psychiatric research and education. It publishes the *American Journal of Psychiatry* and *Psychiatric News* monthly.

American Psychological Association (APA)
750 First St. NE
Washington, DC 20002-4242
(202) 336-5500
Web sites: www.apa.org • www.apahelpcenter.org

This professional organization for psychologists aims to advance psychology as a science, as a profession, and as a means of promoting human welfare. It produces the journal *American Psychologist* as well as numerous publications available online, including the monthly newsletter *Monitor on Psychology* and press releases, such as "Suicidal Thoughts Among College Students More Common than Expected." The APA also provides articles, fact sheets, and interactive features such as "Mind/Body Health" for the general public at its Web site.

Anxiety Disorders Association of America (ADAA)
8730 Georgia Ave. Ste. 600
Silver Spring, MD 20910
(240) 485-1035
Web site: www.adaa .org

This organization educates professionals and the public about OCD and other anxiety disorders, helps sufferers find treatment providers and support groups, and encourages research into causes and treatment. Its Web site offers an e-newsletter, message boards, and self-tests.

National Institute of Mental Health (NIMH)
Public Information and Communications Branch
6001 Executive Blvd. Rm. 8184, MSC 9663
Bethesda, MD 20892-9663
(866) 615-6464 or (301) 443-4513
fax: (301) 443-4279
Web site: www.nimh .nih.gov

This federal agency conducts research on mental and behavioral disorders, including studies aimed at developing new treatments. It also offers booklets and fact sheets on specific conditions as well as science news.

Obsessive Compulsive Anonymous (OCA)
PO Box 215
New Hyde Park, NY 11040
(516) 739-0062
Web site: http://obses sivecompulsiveanony mous.org

The OCA sponsors self-help groups across the United States, in Canada, in some European countries, and through conference calls. These groups follow a twelve-step program that is detailed on the Web site and in publications and recordings that the OCA offers.

Obsessive Compulsive Foundation, Inc. (OCF)
PO Box 961029
Boston, MA 02196
(617) 973-5801
fax: (617) 973-5803
Website: www.oc
foundation.org

The many activities of this organization include educating the public and treatment providers about OCD and related disorders, organizing support groups for sufferers, supporting research into causes and treatments, publishing a bimonthly newsletter, and maintaining a list of providers across the United States who treat OCD.

Obsessive-Compulsive Information Center (OCIC)
Madison Institute of Medicine
7617 Mineral Point Rd., Ste. 300
Madison, WI 53717
(608) 827-2470
fax: (608) 827-2479
Web site: www.mim
inc.org/aboutocic.asp

The center offers patient guides and information packets on OCD and related disorders. Librarians answer questions and search the OCIC's article collections to find specific material. Anyone is welcome to request information. Copies of articles can be ordered for a small fee.

FOR FURTHER READING

Books

Jonathan S. Abramowitz and Arthur C. Houts, eds., *Handbook of OCD: Concepts and Controversies.* New York: Springer, 2005.

Martin M. Antony, Christine Purdon, and Laura Summerfeld, eds., *Psychological Treatment of Obsessive Compulsive Disorder: Fundamentals and Beyond.* Washington, DC: American Psychological Association, 2007.

Jo Derisley, Isobel Heyman, Sarah Robinson, and Cynthia Turner, *Breaking Free from OCD: A CBT Guide for Young People and Their Families.* Philadelphia: Jessica Kingsley, 2008.

Dawn Huebner, *What to Do When Your Brain Gets Stuck: A Kid's Guide to Overcoming OCD.* Washington, DC: Magination, 2007.

Bruce M. Hyman and Troy Dufrene, *Coping with OCD: Practical Strategies for Living Well with Obsessive-Compulsive Disorder.* Oakland, CA: New Harbinger, 2008.

Bruce M. Hyman and Cherry Pedrick, *Obsessive-Compulsive Disorder,* Rev. ed. Minneapolis: Twenty-first Century, 2009.

Jared Douglas Kant, *The Thought That Counts: A Firsthand Account of One Teenager's Experience with Obsessive-Compulsive Disorder.* New York: Oxford University Press, 2008.

B.E. Ling, ed., *Obsessive Compulsive Disorder Research.* New York: Nova Science, 2005.

John S. March, *Talking Back to OCD: The Program That Helps Kids and Teens Say "No Way"—and Parents Say "Way to Go."* New York: Guilford, 2006.

Natalie Rompella, *Obsessive-Compulsive Disorder: The Ultimate Teen Guide.* Lanham, MD: Scarecrow, 2009.

Periodicals

Todd Ackerman, "Analyzing What Is, Isn't OCD," *Houston Chronicle*, July 22, 2007.

Brown University Child and Adolescent Psychopharmacology Update, "New Study Data Support PANDAS Hypothesis: A Link Between Streptococcal Infections and OCD," vol. 7, no. 8, August 2005.

Victoria Burt, "Stimulating the Brain: Deep-Brain Stimulators Have Come a Long Way Since the FDA First Approved Them in 1997," *Medical Design*, vol. 8, no. 2, March 2008.

Paul J. Fink, "Conquering OCD," *Clinical Psychiatry News*, vol. 33, no. 4, April 2005.

Deeanna Franklin, "Effective OCD Treatments Largely Overlooked," *Clinical Psychiatry News*, vol. 34, no. 9, September 2006.

Eric Hollander, "New Developments in an Evolving Field," *Psychiatric Times*, vol. 8, no. 22, July 1, 2005.

Joshua Kendall, "Field Guide to the Obsessive-Compulsive: Famously Fussy," *Psychology Today*, vol. 41, no. 2, March 2008.

Jeffrey Kluger, "When Worry Hijacks the Brain," *Time*, no. 170, vol. 7, August 13, 2007.

———, "Rewiring the Brain." *Time*, vol. 170, no. 11, September 10, 2007.

Robert T. London, "Helping OCPD Patients Break Free," *Clinical Psychiatry News*, vol. 35, no. 7, July 2007.

Management Today, "People Who Can't Let Go," March 1, 2007.

Mark Rowh, "The ABC's of OCD: Teens Who Have Obsessive-Compulsive Disorder Need Not Suffer in Silence," *Current Health 2, a Weekly Reader Publication*, vol. 33, no. 8, April 2007.

Abby Sher, "Diary of a Breakdown," *Self*, vol. 29, no. 5, May 2007.

Lauren Slater, "Who Holds the Clicker? Neuroscientists Hope That Brain Implants Can Treat Intractable Mental Illness. But Can the Circuitry of Despair Be Pinpointed? And Who Would Control These Brave New Minds?" *Mother Jones*, vol. 30, no. 6, November 2005.

Michele G. Sullivan, "Cognitive-Behavioral Therapy Effective for OCD," *Clinical Psychiatry News*, vol. 34, no. 1, January 2006.

Richard Tomkins, "Is There a Bit of OCD in Us All?" *Financial Times*, April 3, 2009.

Miriam E. Tucker, "Medical Costs Higher in OCD than Depression," *International Medicine News*, vol. 41, no. 10, May 15, 2008.

Rick VanBuren, "U. Pittsburgh: More Students Taking Medication for Psychiatric Disorders," *America's Intelligence Wire*, May 24, 2006.

INDEX